The Company They Kept
Volume II

Writers on Unforgettable Friendships

The Company They Kept
Volume II

Writers on Unforgettable Friendships

EDITED AND WITH A PREFACE BY
Robert B. Silvers

NEW YORK REVIEW BOOKS

New York

THE COMPANY THEY KEPT VOLUME II
WRITERS ON UNFORGETTABLE FRIENDSHIPS

Copyright © 2011 by The New York Review of Books
Preface © 2011 Robert B. Silvers
All pieces © by individual authors:

Anna Akhmatova on Osip Mandelstam reprinted with permission of
the estate of the author and with permission of the translator.
Virgil Thomson on Gertrude Stein reprinted with permission of
the Virgil Thomson Foundation, Ltd., copyright owner.
Jonathan Miller on Lenny Bruce reprinted with permission of the author.
Robert Lowell on John Berryman: "For John Berryman" from *Collected Poems* by Robert Lowell.
Copyright © 2003 by Harriet Lowell and Sheridan Lowell.
Reprinted with permission of Farrar Straus and Giroux, LLC.
Stephen Spender on W. H. Auden reprinted with kind permission of the Estate of Stephen Spender.
Mary McCarthy on Hannah Arendt reprinted with permission of the Mary McCarthy Literary Trust.
James Merrill on Elizabeth Bishop: "Elizabeth Bishop (1911-1979)" from *Collected Prose* by James Merrill,
edited by J. D. McClatchy & Stephen Yenser, copyright © 2004 by the Literary Estate of James Merrill at
Washington University. Used by permission of Alfred A. Knopf, a division of Random House, Inc.
Isaiah Berlin on Boris Pasternak and Anna Akhmatova reproduced by arrangement with Curtis Brown Group Ltd.
Joseph Brodsky on Nadezhda Mandelstam: "Nadezhda Mandelstam (1899-1980)" from
Less Than One by Joseph Brodsky. Reprinted by permission of Farrar, Straus and Giroux, LLC.
John Richardson on Douglas Cooper reprinted with permission of The Wylie Agency.
Hector Bianciotti on Jorge Luis Borges reprinted with permission of the author.
Gore Vidal on Dawn Powell reprinted with permission of Janklow & Nesbit Associates.
Bruce Chatwin on George Ortiz reprinted with permission of Aitken Alexander Associates.
Philip Roth on Ivan Klíma from "A Conversation in Prague with Ivan Klíma" from *SHOP TALK: A Writer and
His Colleagues and their Work* by Philip Roth. Copyright © 2001 by Philip Roth. Used by permission of The
Wylie Agency, Houghton Mifflin Harcourt Publishing Company (U.S.) and Vintage Books/The Random House
Group Ltd. (U.K.). All rights reserved.
Elena Bonner on Andrei Sakharov reprinted with permission and with permission of the translator.
Elizabeth Hardwick on Murray Kempton reprinted with permission of the estate of Elizabeth Hardwick.
Aileen Kelly on Isaiah Berlin reprinted with permission of the author.
Murray Kempton on Frank Sinatra reprinted with permission.
Adam Michnik on Zbigniew Herbert reprinted with permission of the author and the translator.
John Updike on Saul Steinberg: "A Tribute to Saul Steinberg"
from *Due Consideration: Essays and Criticisms* by John Updike, copyright © 2007 by John Updike.
Used by permission of Alfred A. Knopf, a division of Random House, Inc.
Jonathan Mirsky on Noel Annan reprinted with permission of the author.
Alison Lurie on Edward Gorey reprinted with permission of Melanie Jackson Agency, LLC.
Ian Buruma on John Schlesinger reprinted with permission of The Wylie Agency.
Darryl Pinckney on Elizabeth Hardwick reprinted with permission of the author.
Colin Thubron on Patrick Leigh Fermor reprinted with permission of the author.

All reasonable attempts have been made to contact the proper copyright holders.
If insufficient credit has been shown please contact the Publisher for proper citation in all future editions.

Published by The New York Review of Books, 435 Hudson Street, Suite 300, New York NY 10014
www.nyrb.com
Distributed in the United States by Random House

Library of Congress Cataloging-in-Publication Data

Writers on unforgettable friendships : the company they kept, Vol. II / edited and with a preface by
Robert B. Silvers.
p. cm. — (New York Review Books collections)
ISBN 978-1-59017-487-6 (alk. paper)
1. Authors—Biography. 2. Friendship. I. Silvers, Robert B. II. Title: Company they kept, Vol. II : writers on
unforgettable friendships.
PN453.W77 2011
809—dc22
[B]
2011003598

ISBN 978-1-59017-487-6

Cover design: Megan Wilson
Printed in the United States of America on acid-free paper

1 3 5 7 9 10 8 6 4 2

Contents

Preface

FOR MANY OF the writers collected here, there was something urgent, even uncontainable, about the need to recall a friend. Behind what they wrote there were often years of intimacy, moments of intense collaboration, and sometimes danger and risk. If there is an invisible, tragic core to this collection, it can be found in Isaiah Berlin's account of the day Stalin called Boris Pasternak in Moscow and asked him two things: whether he was present when Osip Mandelstam recently recited a mocking poem about Stalin to a group, and whether he considered Mandelstam a "master." Pasternak replied that he admired Mandelstam's poetry but had no affection for it and that this, in any case, "was not the point at all." What matters most, Pasternak said, was that it was indispensable that he meet with Stalin; that they must "speak about ultimate issues, about life and death."

"If I were Mandelstam's friend," Stalin said, "I should have known better how to defend him," and he put down the phone.

Soon after, Mandelstam was sent into exile in Voronej and it was precisely there, Anna Akhmatova wrote in the memoir included here, that a "new sense of spaciousness and breadth" appeared in his verse. In a few years Mandelstam was sent to a camp in Siberia, where he died miserably. The circle of great Russian writers that had included him, Anna Akhmatova, and Pasternak was once again broken. Here we publish Anna Akhmatova's memoir of Mandelstam and Isaiah Berlin's account of his meetings with Pasternak and Akhmatova in Moscow as well as Joseph Brodsky's portrait of Mandelstam's widow, Nadezhda, living on in the city of Pskov on the outskirts of Moscow, a central figure in the lives of harassed poets such as Brodsky, whom she befriended before and after he was himself sent into exile to live in a small hut with a goat for company.

In one of his most powerful essays, he describes Nadezhda as "a woman on the run darting through backwaters and provincial towns of the big empire, settling down in a new place only to take off at the first sign of danger"; and after she wrote her two books of astonishing memoirs—without having taken a single note—he describes how "the intelligentsia, especially in Moscow, went into actual turmoil" over her charges against "many of its illustrious members" of "virtual complicity with the regime."

How different was the American circle of the friends of Robert Lowell and his wife Elizabeth Hardwick, including Mary McCarthy, Hannah Arendt, Elizabeth Bishop, John Berryman, and many others, among them Murray Kempton, for some years the companion of my co-editor Barbara Epstein, who lived one building away from the Lowells on West 67th Street near Central Park. Mary had edited a literary journal with Elizabeth Bishop at Vassar College, but it is the poet James Merrill who writes about visiting Bishop in Brazil and finding her poems written there "more truly radiant than any others written in our lifetime." Mary, after years of friendship with Hannah Arendt, writes that what was "theatrical" about her was "a kind of spontaneous power of being seized by an idea, an emotional presentiment whose vehicle her body then became, like an actor."

Robert Lowell, whose correspondence with Elizabeth Bishop is one of the most moving records of literary friendship we have, writes here of meeting John Berryman for the last time in a New York cafeteria shortly before Berryman committed suicide; and of how Berryman told him, "Cal, I was thinking through lunch that I'll never see you again." In the kind of confession we rarely find in a memoir, Lowell describes how he had "misjudged" Berryman's poems, "rattled by their mannerisms." He later found, he writes, that "no voice now or persona fits in my ear as his. It is poignant, abrasive, anguished, humorous. It is we...who are labored and private while he is smiling."

Of his wife Elizabeth Hardwick—a founder of *The New York Review* and its advisory editor since its first issue—Darryl Pinckney, who studied with her at Barnard College, recalled how she told her students that "there are really only two reasons to write—desperation or revenge." When she brought into her class Pasternak's 1931 memoir, *Safe Conduct*, Darryl describes her reading aloud the passage about Vladimir Mayakovsky's suicide in the Moscow winter:

> When she got to the line about the black velvet of the talent in himself, she stopped and threw herself back in the chair, curls trembling. Either we got it or we didn't, but it was clear from the way she struck her breastbone that to get it was, for her, the gift of life.

Barbara Epstein caught something of Elizabeth when she said, "All air and nerve, like nobody's business." In her essay printed here on Murray Kempton and his collected essays, Elizabeth wrote, in her wonderfully compressed prose, that "part of his refinement was to be generous to the thieving and polite to the fastidious." She quotes Murray's estimate of the jailed Wall Street trader Michael Milken:

"However we may despair of touching the infinite, we never so sense its presence as when we contemplate the sincerity of the swindler."

We publish here Murray's own impressions of Frank Sinatra, who told Milton Berle that "the only way you learn to sing is to listen to Billie Holliday and find out how to play out a note"—a piece of advice that might be taken as a theme, with many variations, of this collection. I'm grateful to Angela Hederman for her work in bringing together these memoirs from the *Review*, with the webs of genius we can glimpse among them.

—Robert B. Silvers

I

ANNA AKHMATOVA

ON OSIP MANDELSTAM

This portrait of Osip Mandelstam is a condensation of a long and rather rough fragment from the memoirs of the poet Anna Akhmatova.

MANDELSTAM WAS ONE of the most brilliant conversationalists. In conversing he didn't listen to himself, nor did he answer himself as almost everyone does today; he was considerate, imaginative, and infinitely varied. I have never heard him repeat himself. Osip Emilievitch could learn foreign languages with extraordinary ease. He recited by heart in Italian whole pages out of the *Divine Comedy*. Not long before his death, he had asked his wife Nadezhda to teach him English, which he didn't know at all. He spoke about poetry dazzlingly, often in a prejudiced way, and sometimes he was monstrously unjust—about Blok for example. About Pasternak he said: "I am thinking about him so much that it even makes me feel tired." And also, "I am sure he has never read a single line of mine." About Marina: "I am an anti-Tsvetayevist." He was at home with music and this for a poet is extremely rare. More than anything else, he feared the loss of his poetic voice. When this happened, he rushed around in a state of terror and he invented all sorts of absurd reasons to explain this calamity. A second, frequent cause of distress was his readership. It always seemed to him that he was liked by the wrong readers. He knew well and remembered other poets' poems, sometimes falling in love with a single line. He could memorize with ease poems which were read to him.

I met Mandelstam in the Spring of 1911, at Viatcheslav Tvanov's "Tower."[1] He was then a thin young boy with a twig of lily-of-the-valley in his buttonhole, his head thrown up and back, with eyelashes so long that they covered half his cheek.

Throughout the 'Teens we frequently met at various literary occasions. These were very important years for Mandelstam as a writer. There is yet much thinking to be done, much to be said about these formative years. Mandelstam greeted the Revolution as a completely mature poet, and a well-known one, at least in a small circle.

I saw Mandelstam especially often in 1914-1917, in Petersburg. He would come by for me with a rented carriage, and we rode over the unbelievable holes of the revolutionary winter, among the famous bonfires which burnt as late as May, listening to the sound of rifle-shooting rushing towards us, we didn't know from where. Mandelstam was one of the first to write poems on civic themes. For him, the Revolution was an enormous event, and it is not by chance that the word *people* appears in his verse. In March of 1917, Mandelstam disappeared. At that time people disappeared and reappeared and no one was surprised by it. In Moscow he was becoming a permanent contributor to a magazine entitled *The Flag of Labor*.

In the summer of 1924 Osip Mandelstam brought to me his young wife, Nadezhda. I was then living on Fontanka Street, No. 2. Nadezhda was what the French call "*laide mais délicieuse*." Our friendship

---

1. A famous Symbolist literary salon in pre-Revolutionary St. Petersburg where an esoteric *fin-de-siécle* atmosphere prevailed.

started on that day, and it has lasted to this day. Osip loved Nadezhda extraordinarily, incredibly much. He didn't let her out of his sight, he didn't allow her to work, he was wildly jealous, he asked her for advice about every word in his poems. Altogether, I have never seen anything like it in all of my life.

In the Fall of 1933, Mandelstam was finally allocated an apartment in Moscow (which he celebrated in his poems). It looked as if the vagabond life which took the Mandelstams back and forth between Leningrad and Moscow had ended. For the first time Osip started to collect books, mostly ancient editions of Italian poets. At that time he was translating Petrarch. But in fact things remained unsettled. Mandelstam had to phone somewhere all the time, he waited and hoped and nothing ever came of it. There was no money at all, and only half-promises for reviewing and translating jobs. Although the times were relatively bloodless[2] the shadow of disaster and doom hung over this house. About that time, Mandelstam changed physically a great deal: he became heavier, his hair turned gray, he had trouble breathing. He looked like an old man (he was forty-two) but his eyes continued to sparkle. His poetry was becoming better all the time; so was his prose.

On May 30th, 1934 he was arrested. On that very day, after a deluge of telegrams and telephone calls, I arrived at the Mandelstams from Leningrad. We were then all so poor that in order to be able to buy a return ticket, I took a statuette with me to sell, a 1924 Danko. The warrant for Mandelstam's arrest was signed by Yagoda[3] himself. All night the police searched the apartment. They were looking for poems. We all sat in one room. It was very quiet. Behind the wall, at

---

2. Akhmatova writes "vegetarian," which has the same literal meaning in Russian as in English.

3. The chief of the Soviet Secret police at that time.

Kirsanov's[4], we could hear a Hawaiian guitar. The detective found *The Century of the Wolf* and showed it to Osip Emilievitch, who nodded his head in silence. He was taken away at seven o'clock, when it was already daylight. He kissed me when we parted.

Fifteen days later, early in the morning, Nadezhda had a phone call and was told to be at the Kazan railroad station that night if she wanted to accompany her husband in exile. It was all over. Our friend X and I went around collecting money for the trip. People gave a lot. Mrs. B. burst into tears and stuffed into my hand without counting it, a whole lot of money.

I went to the Kazan station with Nadezhda, but my own train was leaving from the Leningrad station early that evening, and Osip was brought out only after I had left the Kazan station. No one was allowed to speak with him. It was too bad that I hadn't waited for him, and he hadn't seen me, because later on, when he had fits of insanity, he was persuaded that I had surely been shot, and kept looking for my corpse.

In February of 1936, I went to visit Mandelstam in Voronej and learned all the details of his "affair." It is striking that a sense of spaciousness and breadth appeared in Mandelstam's verse precisely in Voronej, when he was not at all free.

It was there that he was forced, for ambiguous reasons, to give a lecture about Acmeism. It mustn't be forgotten that he had said in 1937, "I do not disavow the living or the dead."

There have been several gossipy, ill-informed books about Mandelstam published in recent years. One is Georges Ivanov's *Petersburg Nights*. Even more shocking in its inaccuracies and trivialities is a book by Leonid Chatsky, published under the aegis of the best, oldest American university, Harvard!

---

4. A Soviet poet, younger than Mandelstam, who is still alive today.

Mandelstam was a tragic figure. Even while in exile in Voronej, he wrote works of untold beauty and power. And he had no poetic forerunners—wouldn't that be something worth thinking about for his biographers? In all of world poetry, I know of no other such case. We know the sources of Pushkin and Blok, but who will tell us where that new, divine harmony, Mandelstam's poetry, came from?

I last saw Mandelstam in the Fall of 1937. He and Nadezhda had come to Leningrad for a couple of days. The times were apocalyptic. Disaster was following in the footsteps of each of us. Mandelstam had no money whatever. He and his wife had no place to live. Osip breathed heavily; he was catching air with his lips. I came to meet him, I do not remember where. Everything was like a frightening dream. Someone who arrived after me said that Osip's father had no warm clothes. Osip took off the sweater he was wearing under his jacket and gave it to pass on to his father. At that time we were reading simultaneously Joyce's *Ulysses*—he in a good German translation, I in the original. Several times we started to talk about *Ulysses*, but we couldn't—it was not a time to talk about books.

Mandelstam was arrested for a second and last time on May 2nd, 1938. He died a few months later in Siberia.

Adapted by Olga Andreyev Carlisle
—December 23, 1965

2

VIRGIL THOMSON
ON GERTRUDE STEIN

GERTRUDE STEIN IN her younger days had liked to write all night and
sleep all day. She also, it seems, ate copiously, drank wine, and
smoked cigars. By the time I knew her, at fifty-two, she ate abstemi-
ously; she neither drank nor smoked; and she was likely to wake, as
people do in middle life, by nine. Her volume had been diminished
too. Her appearance, nevertheless, on account of low stature (five
feet, two), remained monumental, like that of some saint or sybil
sculpted three-fourths life size. Her working powers also were intact,
remained so, indeed, until her death at seventy-two.

Actually a whole domestic routine had been worked out for encouraging those powers to function daily. In the morning she would
read, write letters, play with the dog, eventually bathe, dress, and
have her lunch. In the afternoon she drove in the car, walked, window-
shopped, spent a little money. She did nothing by arrangement till
after four. At some point in her day she always wrote; and since she
waited always for the moment when she would be full of readiness to
write, what she wrote came out of fullness as an overflowing.

Year round, these routines varied little, except that in the country,
if there were houseguests, excursions by car might be a little longer,
tea or lunch taken out instead of at home. When alone and not at

work, Gertrude would walk, read, or meditate. She loved to walk; and she consumed books by the dozen, sent to her when away from home by the American Library in Paris. She read English and American history, memoirs, minor literature from the nineteenth century, and crime fiction, rarely modern artwriting, and never the commercial magazines. When people were around she would talk and listen, ask questions. She talked with anybody and everybody. When exchanging news and views with neighbors, concierges, policemen, shop people, garage men, hotel servants, she was thoroughly interested in them all. Gertrude not only liked people, she needed them. They were grist for her poetry, a relief from the solitudes of a mind essentially introspective.

Alice Toklas neither took life easy nor fraternized casually. She got up at six and cleaned the drawing room herself, because she did not wish things broken. (Porcelain and other fragile objects were her delight, just as pictures were Gertrude's; and she could imagine using violence toward a servant who might break one.) She liked being occupied, anyway, and did not need repose, ever content to serve Gertrude or be near her. She ran the house, ordered the meals, cooked on occasion, and typed out everything that got written into the blue copybooks that Gertrude had adopted from French school children. From 1927 or '28 she also worked petit point, matching in silk the colors and shades of designs made especially for her by Picasso. These tapestries were eventually applied to a pair of Louis XV small armchairs (*chauffeuses*) that Gertrude had bought for her. She was likely, any night, to go to bed by eleven, while Miss Stein would sit up late if there were someone to talk with.

Way back before World War I, in 1910 or so, in Granada, Gertrude had experienced the delights of writing directly in the landscape. This does not mean just working out of doors; it means being surrounded by the thing one is writing about at the time one is writing about it. Later, in 1924, staying at Saint-Rémy in Provence, and sitting in fields beside the irrigation ditches, she found the same sound of running water as in Granada to soothe her while she wrote or while she simply sat, imbuing herself with the landscape's sight and sound. In the country around Belley, where she began to summer only a few years later, she wrote *Lucy Church Amiably* wholly to the sound of streams and waterfalls.

Bravig Imbs, an American poet and novelist who knew her in the late Twenties, once came upon her doing this. The scene took place in a field, its enactors being Gertrude, Alice, and a cow. Alice, by means of a stick, would drive the cow around the field. Then, at a sign from Gertrude, the cow would be stopped; and Gertrude would write in her copybook. After a bit, she would pick up her folding stool and progress to another spot, whereupon Alice would again start the cow moving around the field till Gertrude signaled she was ready to write again. Though Alice now says that Gertrude drove the cow, she waiting in the car, the incident, whatever its choreography, reveals not only Gertrude's working intimacy with landscape but also the concentration of two friends on an act of composition by one of them that typifies and reveals their daily life for forty years. Alice had decided long before that "Gertrude was always right," that she was to have whatever she wanted when she wanted it, and that the way to keep herself always wanted was to keep Gertrude's writing always and forever unhindered, unopposed.

Gertrude's preoccupation with painting and painters was not shared by Alice except in so far as certain of Gertrude's painter friends touched her heart, and Picasso was almost the only one of these. Juan Gris was another, and Christian Bérard a very little bit. But Matisse I know she had not cared for, nor Braque. If it had not been for Gertrude, I doubt that Alice would ever have had much to do with the world of painting. She loved objects and furniture, practiced cooking and gardening, understood music. Of music, indeed, she had a long experience, having once, as a young girl, played a piano concerto in public. But painting was less absorbing to her than to Gertrude.

Gertrude's life with pictures seems to have begun as a preoccupation shared with her brothers, Michael and Leo. The sculptor Jacques Lipschitz once remarked to me the miraculous gift of perception by which these young Californians, in Paris of the 1900s, had gone straight to the cardinal values. Virtually without technical experience (since only Leo, among them, had painted at all) and without advice (for there were no modern-art scholars then), they bought Cézanne, Matisse, and Picasso. In quantity and, of course, for almost nothing. But also, according to Lipschitz, the Steins' taste was strongest when they bought together. Gertrude and Leo did this as long as they lived together, which was till about 1911. Michael, who had started quite early buying Matisses, kept that up till World War I. After Gertrude and Leo separated, she made fewer purchases and no major ones at all, save some Juan Gris canvases that represented a continuing commitment to Spanish cubism and to friendship. She could no longer buy Picasso or Cézanne after their prices got high, or after she owned a car. But throughout the Twenties and Thirties she was always looking for new painters, without being able to commit herself to any of them till she discovered about 1929 Sir Francis Rose. From him she quickly acquired nearly a hundred pictures, and she insisted till her death that he was a great painter. No other collector, no museum, no international dealer has yet gone so far.

Looking at painting had been for Gertrude Stein a nourishment throughout the late twenties and thirties of her own life. She never ceased to state her debt to Cézanne, for it was from constantly gazing on a portrait by him that she had found her way into and through the vast maze of motivations and proclivities that make up the patterns of people and types of people in *Three Lives* and in *The Making of*

Americans. "The wonderful thing about Cézanne," she would say, "is that he was never tempted." Gertrude Stein's biographers have stated that Picasso also was a source for her and that in *Tender Buttons* she was endeavoring to reproduce with words the characteristic devices of cubist painting. There may even be in existence a quotation from Gertrude herself to this effect. But she certainly did not repeat it in the way she loved to repeat her allegiance to Cézanne. I myself have long doubted the validity, or at any rate the depth, of such a statement. An influence of poetry on painting is quite usual, a literary theme being illustrated by images. But any mechanism by which this procedure might be reversed and painting come to influence literature (beyond serving as subject for a review) is so rare a concept that the mere statement of Gertrude Stein's intent to receive such an influence surely requires fuller explanation. Let us try.

First of all, *Tender Buttons*, subtitled *Objects . . . Food . . . Rooms*, is an essay in description, of which the subjects are those commonly employed by painters of still life. And cubist painting too was concerned with still life. Cubism's characteristic device in representing still life was to eliminate the spatially fixed viewpoint, to see around corners, so to speak, to reduce its subject to essentials of form and profile and then to reassemble these as a summary or digest of its model. Resemblance was not forbidden; on the contrary, clues were offered to help the viewer recognize the image; and cubist painters (from the beginning, according to Gertrude) had been disdainful of viewers who could not "read" their canvases. (Today's "abstract" painters, on the other hand, maintain that in their work resemblances are purely accidental.)

According to Alice Toklas, the author's aim in *Tender Buttons* was "to describe something without mentioning it." Sometimes the name of the object is given in a title, sometimes not; but each description is full of clues, some of them easy to follow up, others put there for throwing you off the scent. All are legitimately there, however, since in Blake's words, "everything possible to be believed is an image of truth," and since in Gertrude Stein's method anything that comes to one in a moment of concentrated working is properly a part of the poem. Nevertheless, unveiling the concealed image is somewhat more difficult to a reader of *Tender Buttons* than to the viewer of a cubist still life. For a still life is static; nothing moves in it; time is arrested. In literature, on the other hand, one word comes after another and the whole runs forward. To have produced static pictures in spite of a non-fixed eyepoint was cubism's triumph, just as giving the illusion of movement within a framed picture was the excitement of vorticism, as in Marcel Duchamp's "Nude Descending a Staircase." To have described objects, food, and rooms both statically and dynamically, with both a painter's eye and a poet's continuity, gives to *Tender Buttons* its particular brilliance, its way of both standing still and moving forward.

Now the carrier of that motion, make no mistake, is a rolling eloquence in no way connected with cubism. This eloquence, in fact, both carries forward the description and defeats it, just as in cubist painting description was eventually defeated by the freedom of the painter (with perspective making no demands) merely to create a composition. Cubism was always, therefore, in danger of going decorative (hence flat); and the kind of writing I describe here could just as easily turn into mere wit and oratory. That cubism was something of an impasse its short life, from 1909 to 1915, would seem to indicate; and there were never more than two possible exits from it. One was complete concealment of the image, hence in effect its elimination; the other was retreat into naturalism. Both paths have been followed in our time, though not by Picasso, who has avoided abstraction as just another trap leading to the decorative, and who could never bring himself, for mere depiction, to renounce the ironic attitudes involved in voluntary stylization.

Gertrude, faced with two similar paths, chose both. During the years between 1927 and '31, she entered into an involvement with naturalism that produced at the end of her life *Yes Is for a Very Young Man, Brewsie and Willie,* and *The Mother of Us All,* each completely clear and in no way mannered. She was also during those same years pushing abstraction farther than it had ever gone before, not only in certain short pieces still completely hermetic (even to Alice Toklas), but in extended studies of both writing and feeling in which virtually everything remains obscure but the mood, works such as *As a Wife Has a Cow, a Love Story; Patriarchal Poetry;* and *Stanzas in Meditation.*

Her last operas and plays are in the humane tradition of letters, while her monumental abstractions of the late 1920s and early 1930s are so intensely aware of both structure and emotion that they may well be the origin of a kind of painting that came later to be known as "abstract expressionism." If this be true, then Gertrude Stein, after borrowing from cubism a painting premise, that of the non-fixed viewpoint, returned that premise to its origins, transformed. Whether the transformation could have been operated within painting itself, without the help of a literary example, we shall never know, because the literary example was there. We do know, however, that no single painter either led that transformation or followed it through as a completed progress in his own work.

Gertrude had been worried about painting ever since cubism had ceased to evolve. She did not trust abstraction in art, which she found constricted between flat color schemes and pornography. Surrealism, for her taste, was too arbitrary as to theme and too poor as painting. And she could not give her faith to the neo-Romantics either, though she found Bérard "alive" and "the best" of them. She actually decided in 1928 that "painting [had] become a minor art again," meaning without nourishment for her. Then within the year, she had found Francis Rose. What nourishment she got from him I cannot dream; nor did she ever speak of him save as a gifted one destined to lead his art—an English leader this time, instead of Spanish.

In her work, during these late Twenties, while still developing ideas received from Picasso, she was also moving into new fields opened by her friendship with me. I do not wish to pretend that her ventures into romantic feeling, into naturalism, autobiography, and the opera came wholly through me, though her discovery of the opera as a poetic form certainly did. Georges Hugnet, whom I had brought to her, was at least equally a stimulation, as proved by her "translation" of one of his extended works. She had not previously accepted, since youth, the influence of any professional writer. Her early admiration for Henry James and Mark Twain had long since become a reflex. She still remembered Shakespeare of the sonnets, as *Stanzas in Meditation* will show; and she considered Richardson's *Clarissa Harlowe* (along with *The Making of Americans*) to be "the other great novel in English." But for "movements" and their organizers in contemporary poetry she had the greatest disdain—for Pound, Eliot, Yeats, and their volunteer militiamen. She admitted Joyce to be "a good writer," disclaimed any influence on her from his work, and believed, with some evidence, that she had influenced him.

She knew that in the cases of Sherwood Anderson and Ernest Hemingway her influence had gone to them, not theirs to her. I do not know the real cause of her break with Hemingway, only that after a friendship of several years she did not see him any more and declared forever after that he was "yellow." Anderson remained a friend always, though I do not think she ever took him seriously as a writer. The poet Hart Crane she did take seriously. And there were French young men, René Crevel, for one, whom she felt tender about and whom Alice adored. Cocteau amused her as a wit and as a dandy, less so as an organizer of epochs, a role she had come to hold in little respect from having known in prewar times Guillaume Apollinaire, whom she esteemed low as a poet, even lower as a profiteer of cubism. Pierre de Massot she respected as a prose master; but he was too French, too violent, to touch her deeply. Gide and Jouhandeau, making fiction out of sex, she found as banal as any titillater of chambermaids. Max Jacob she had disliked personally from the time of his early friendship with Picasso. I never heard her express any opinion of him as a writer, though Alice says now that she admired him.

In middle life she had come at last to feel about her own work that it "could be compared to the great poetry of the past." And if she was nearly alone during her lifetime in holding this view (along with Alice Toklas, myself, and perhaps a very few more), she was equally alone in having almost no visible poetic parents or progeny. Her writing seemed to come from nowhere and to influence, at that time, none but reporters and novelists. She herself, considering the painter Cézanne her chief master, believed that under his silent tutelage a major message had jumped like an electric arc from painting to poetry. And she also suspected that its high tension was in process of short-circuiting again, from her through me, this time to music. I do not offer this theory as my own, merely as a thought thrown out by Gertrude Stein to justify, perhaps, by one more case the passing of an artistic truth or method, which she felt strongly to have occurred for her, across one of those sensory distances that lie between sight, sound, and words.

There was nevertheless, in Alice Toklas, literary influence from a nonprofessional source. As early as 1910, in a narrative called "Ada," later published in *Geography and Plays*, a piece which recounts Miss Toklas's early life, Gertrude imitated Alice's way of telling a story.

This sentence is typical: "He had a pleasant life while he was living and after he was dead his wife and children remembered him." Condensation in this degree was not Gertrude's way; expansion through repetition (what she called her "garrulity") was more natural to her. But she could always work from an auditory model, later in *Brewsie and Willie* transcribing almost literally the usage and syntax of World War II American soldiers. And having mastered a new manner by imitating Alice Toklas in *Ada*, she next mixed it with her repetitive manner in a story called "Miss Furr and Miss Skeen." Then she set aside the new narrative style for nearly thirty years.

In 1933 she took it up again for writing *The Autobiography of Alice B. Toklas*, which is the story of her own life told in Miss Toklas's words. This book is in every way except actual authorship Alice Toklas's book; it reflects her mind, her language, her private view of Gertrude, also her unique narrative powers. Every story in it is told as Alice herself had always told it. And when in 1961 Miss Toklas herself wrote *What Is Remembered*, she told her stories with an even greater brevity. There is nothing comparable to this compactness elsewhere in English, nor to my knowledge in any other literature save possibly in Julius Caesar's *De Bello Gallico*. Gertrude imitated it three times with striking success. She could not use it often, because its way was not hers.

Her own way with narrative was ever elliptical, going into slow orbit around her theme. Alice's memory and interests were visual; she could recall forever the exact costumes people had worn, where they had stood or sat, the décor of a room, the choreography of an occasion. Gertrude's memory was more for the sound of a voice, for accent, grammar, and vocabulary. And even these tended to grow vague in one day, because her sustained curiosity about what had happened lay largely in the possibilities of any incident for revealing character.

How often have I heard her begin some tale, a recent one or a far-away one, and then as she went on with it get first repetitive and then uncertain till Alice would look up over the tapestry frame and say, "I'm sorry, Lovey; it wasn't like that at all." "All right, Pussy," Gertrude would say. "You tell it." Every story that ever came into the house eventually got told in Alice's way, and this was its definitive version. The accounts of life in the country between 1942 and 1945 that make up *Wars I Have Seen* seem to me, on the other hand, Gertrude's own; I find little of Alice in them. Then how are they so vivid? Simply from the fact, or at least so I imagine, that she would write in the evening about what she had seen that day, describe events while their memory was still fresh.

Gertrude's artistic output has the quality, rare in our century, of continuous growth. Picasso had evolved rapidly through one discovery after another until the cubist time was over. At that point, in 1915, he was only thirty-three and with a long life to be got through. He has got through it on sheer professionalism—by inventing tricks and using them up (tricks mostly recalling the history of art or evoking historic Spanish art), by watching the market very carefully (collecting his own pictures), and by keeping himself advised about trends in literary content and current-events content. But his major painting was all done early. Igor Stravinsky followed a similar pattern. After giving to the world between 1909 and 1913 three proofs of colossally expanding power—*The Firebird, Petrouchka*, and *The Rite of Spring*—he found himself at thirty-one unable to expand farther. And since, like Picasso, he was still to go on living, and since he could not imagine living without making music, he too was faced with an unhappy choice. He could either make music out of his own past (which he disdained to do) or out of music's past (which he is still doing). For both men, when expansion ceased, working methods became their subject.

One could follow this design through many careers in music, painting, and poetry. Pound, I think, continued to develop; Eliot, I should say, did not. Arnold Schoenberg was in constant evolution his chief pupils. Alban Berg and Anton Webern, were more static. The last two were saved by early death from possible decline of inspiration, just as James Joyce's approaching blindness concentrated and extended his high period for twenty years, till he had finished two major works, *Ulysses* and *Finnegans Wake*. He died fulfilled, exhausted, but lucky in the sense that constant growth had not been expected of him. Indeed, for all that the second of these two works is more complex than the first, both in concept and in language, it does not represent a growth in anything but mastery. Joyce was a virtuoso type, like Picasso, of whom Max Jacob, Picasso's friend from earliest youth, had said, "Always he escapes by acrobatics." And virtuosos do not grow; they merely become more skillful. At least they do not grow like vital organisms, but rather, like crystals, reproduce their characteristic forms.

Gertrude Stein's maturation was more like that of Arnold Schoenberg. She ripened steadily, advanced slowly from each stage to the next. She had started late, after college and medical school. From *Three Lives*, begun in 1904 at thirty, through *The Making of Americans*, finished in 1911, her preoccupation is character analysis. From *Tender Buttons* (1912) to *Patriarchal Poetry* (1927) a quite different kind of writing is presented (not, of course, without having been prefigured). This is hermetic to the last degree, progressing within its fifteen-year duration from picture-words and rolling rhetoric to syntactical complexity and neutral words. From 1927 to 1934 two things go on at once. There are long hermetic works (*Four Saints*, *Lucy Church Amiably*, and *Stanzas in Meditation*) but also straightforward ones like *The Autobiography of Alice B. Toklas* and the lectures on writing. After her return in 1935 from the American lecture tour, hermetic writing gradually withers and the sound of spoken English becomes her theme, giving in *Yes Is for a Very Young Man*, in *The Mother of Us All*, and in *Brewsie and Willie* vernacular portraits of remarkable veracity.

Her development had not been aided or arrested by public success, of which there had in fact been very little. The publication of *Three Lives* in 1909 she had subsidized herself, as she did in 1922 that of the miscellany, *Geography and Plays*. *The Making of Americans*, published by Robert McAlmon's Contact Editions in 1925, was her first book-size book to be issued without her paying for it; and she was over fifty. She had her first bookstore success at fifty-nine with the *Autobiography*. When she died in 1946, at seventy-two, she had been working till only a few months before without any diminution of power. Her study of technical problems never ceased; never had she felt obliged to fabricate an inspiration; and she never lost her ability to speak from the heart.

Gertrude lived by the heart, indeed; and domesticity was her theme. Not for her the matings and rematings that went on among the Amazons. An early story from 1903, published after her death, *Things as They Are*, told of one such intrigue in post-Radcliffe days. But after 1907 her love life was serene, and it was Alice Toklas who made it so. Indeed, it was this tranquil life that offered to Gertrude a fertile soil of sentiment-security in which other friendships great and small could come to flower, wither away, be watered, cut off, or preserved in a book. Her life was like that of a child, to whom danger can come only from the outside, never from home, and whose sole urgency is growth. It was also that of an adult who demanded all the rights of a man along with the privileges of a woman.

Just as Gertrude kept up friendships among the Amazons, though she did not share their lives, she held certain Jews in attachment for their family-like warmth, though she felt no solidarity with Jewry.

Tristan Tzara—French-language poet from Roumania, Dada pioneer, early surrealist, and battler for the Communist party—she said was "like a cousin." Miss Etta and Dr. Claribel Cone, picture buyers and friends from Baltimore days, she handled almost as if they were her sisters. The sculptors Jo Davidson and Jacques Lipschitz, the painter Man Ray she accepted as though they had a second cousin's right to be part of her life. About men or goyim, even about her oldest man friend, Picasso, she could feel unsure; but a woman or a Jew she could size up quickly. She accepted without cavil, indeed, all the conditionings of her Jewish background. And if, as she would boast, she was "a bad Jew," she at least did not think of herself as Christian. Of heaven and salvation and all that she would say, "When a Jew dies he's dead." We used to talk a great deal, in fact, about our very different religious conditionings, the subject having come up through my remarking the frequency with which my Jewish friends would break with certain of theirs and then never make up. Gertrude's life had contained many people that she still spoke of (Mabel Dodge, for instance) but from whom she refused all communication. The Stettheimers' conversation was also full of references to people they had known well but did not wish to know any more. And I began to imagine this definitiveness about separations as possibly a Jewish trait. I was especially struck by Gertrude's rupture with her brother Leo, with whom she had lived for many years in intellectual and no doubt affectionate communion, but to whom she never spoke again after they had divided their pictures and furniture, taken up separate domiciles.

The explanation I offered for such independent behavior was that the Jewish religion, though it sets aside a day for private Atonement, offers no mechanics for forgiveness save for offenses against one's own patriarch, and even he is not obliged to pardon. When a Christian, on the other hand, knows he has done wrong to anyone, he is obliged in all honesty to attempt restitution; and the person he has wronged must thereupon forgive. So that if Jews seem readier to quarrel than to make up, that fact seems possibly to be the result of their having no confession-and-forgiveness formula, whereas Christians, who experience none of the embarrassment that Jews find in admitting misdeeds, arrange their lives, in consequence, with greater flexibility, though possibly, to a non-Christian view, with less dignity.

Gertrude liked this explanation, and for nearly twenty years it remained our convention. It was not till after her death that Alice said one day,

> You and Gertrude had it settled between you as to why Jews don't make up their quarrels, and I went along with you. But now I've found a better reason for it. Gertrude was right, of course, to believe that "when a Jew dies he's dead." And that's exactly why Jews don't need to make up. When we've had enough of someone we can get rid of him. You Christians can't, because you've got to spend eternity together.

—July 7, 1966

3

JONATHAN MILLER
ON LENNY BRUCE

IT IS HARD to write fairly about Lenny Bruce now that he's dead. At least it is difficult to be just, in the way that he, in his more realistic moments, might have preferred. For Bruce became an issue in the last years of his life. He became the focus of controversy between opposing vested interests, neither of which really gave a damn for the man himself. The complementary roles of mascot and victim proved inevitably fatal, and through a strange mixture of simple-minded vanity and courageous generosity he lived up too thoroughly to a public personality partly supplied by his sponsors and tormentors. In the end it led quite inexorably to an ordeal which both sides, with different types of satisfaction, saw coming a long way off. The villains of the piece were all those thick-necked hypocritical authorities who hounded him down, in state after state, until he was finally too poor, too weak, and too confused to survive. All along he was up against a brutal, prejudiced society which somehow seemed unable to afford the easy conversational freedom that Bruce offered to his audiences. But we, his sponsors, his eager fluting publicists, must also bear some of the responsibility for the way things turned out. Bruce was in many ways a willing sucker for the sort of martyrdom upon which affluent, free-thinking liberals vicariously thrive. His dreadful ordeal through the courts, destitution, and ultimate death, provided a nice, flourishing proof of the liberals' conviction that the world is cruel, repressed, and indifferent. But Bruce was too ready to sacrifice *himself* on behalf of this demonstration. He was too accommodating, and those of us who supported him in print were sometimes too excited, or else too selfish, to notice that Bruce's uneducated simplicity often led him to yield without criticism to the flattery of over-elaborate interpretation. Underneath all that hipster cool, it is to be remembered that Bruce was rather an innocent bloke, badly read, and so keen to be accepted and admired by educated people that he was sometimes deceived by the over-complicated program which certain missionary intellectuals read into his act. It's possible that he suffered very badly from being taken up quite like this. As intellectual support for his act grew, he began to take seriously all that stuff about being the prophet of a new morality and would replace a lot of his regular material with sententious sermons. He would quote from Doctor Albert Ellis, M.D., recite dubious pharmacological justifications for "pot," and generally became quite boring.

He was so generously open to intellectual flattery, so pleased to discover that he had authoritative support, that he sometimes failed to realize how much he was being used as a dispensable stalking horse for middle-class liberal dares. Strangely enough, by stepping up the dirt in the service of this mission he was to some extent being exploited by a mirror image of the very prejudice which finally hounded him to his death. I can still, with some shame, recall my own euphoric horror at hearing him come out with four-letter words in front of a solid middle class audience at The Establishment in London. It seems contemptible now, the way in which we used him to do our dubious dirty work of evangelical sexual shock therapy. For the marvelous thing about Bruce was not the way in which he deliberately introduced obscenity into his act, though as time went on, with encouragement from us, he did do more and more of this, but the way in which he never held back obscenity if it was relevant to his subject. He spoke to his audience just as most of us speak to each other in private, without feeling that he had any need to button his lip when dealing with pelvic affairs. But we got too zealously worked up on behalf of this particular aspect of his act, and egged him on to fresh excesses of sexual radicalism. Left to himself, I sometimes doubt whether he would have pressed on this point quite so much. But as it is, he rose a bit too eagerly to the bait of our shady approval, and found himself assuming more and more the role of persecuted prophet of a slightly phony gospel. For as Christopher Lasch has pointed out, "by insisting that sex was the highest form of love, the highest form of human discourse, the modern prophets of sex did not so much undermine the prudery against which they appeared to be in rebellion . . . as invert it."

It would be foolish, simply in the light of his painful death, to exonerate Bruce himself altogether from the comparative absurdity of this position. Intellectually underprivileged in several important respects, he was in every other way fully aware and even proud of his participation in the campaign for utopian sexual enlightenment. He did feel, I'm quite sure, that if only prudery would relax we could screw our way to peace and prosperity for all. That in some hypothetical millenium, bigotry and suffering would not be heard for the swishing of the pricks. Perhaps it's significant that it was *Playboy* magazine which serialized his autobiography. Commercially this publication also embodies the half-formed belief that sexual knots alone contort the body politic. Heffner's interminable editorial philosophy often reads like a transcript of one of Bruce's more didactic bits, and the rest of the magazine, too, reverberates with the idea that by being honestly sybaritic human beings will simply forget to be nasty and collapse instead into a voluptuous communion, peacefully noshing on Plumrose Playmates, their savagery soothed by first-class hi-fi. It is sad that Bruce should have allowed himself to be hanged until he was dead from the yard-arm of this particular ship of fools. But he was encouraged to do so by people who were prepared to push a much more sophisticated version of the same argument. I doubt if Lionel Trilling's essay on "Freud and the Crisis of Our Culture" ever got to Bruce's immediate attention, but the general idea was familiar to intellectuals with whom Bruce came in contact. They believed, sincerely, though I think mistakenly, that the biological core of human nature, inaccessible to the repressive threats of culture, offered a life-saver for the individual who found himself drowning in modern life. Without fully wishing to understand the complex institutional history of this proposal, certain intellectuals leaped at its utopian possibilities and then found Bruce a conveniently self-sacrificing public spokesman on behalf of the doctrine.

But that's enough carping. I make it sound as if Bruce was no more than a gullible ass who went down in the name of something completely ludicrous, although even if that were the case there would be a certain pathetic honor in his death. But even if the cause, as fought, was riddled with absurdity, so, of course, were the brutal idiots who considered it important enough to oppose it to the death. Anyway, there was much more to Bruce than that. So that his life and death *are* significant and serious attention must be paid.

Bruce was a great stage artist, a soloist of unbelievable virtuosity. The thousands of people who filled two houses of an old movie theater in Greenwich Village in December 1963 are a witness of that. So were the audiences that came back night after night during his month in London. The people who followed him were charmed by the free conversational directness of the man. He liked his audiences and took great pains to feel his way towards the individual temperament of each one. And if he felt comfortable with a group there was no end to the effort he would make to entertain and delight them. It's not really true that he thrived on hostility, though he sometimes managed to put on a show of hard, glittering verve when the animals were in—people who talked loudly throughout his act, sounding "like tape played backwards." But generally an unfriendly audience made him stiff and defiant, and then he would sometimes become brutally dirty, just for the hell of it. He also had amazing resources of descriptive finesse with which he would reward friendly attention. He had an uncannily accurate ear and a novelist's eye for the sort of crucial visual detail which could suddenly delight spectators with a shock of recognition. Midgets with blue suits and brown boots, hands only visible on the steering wheel of a car, speeding along the Santa Anna freeway; or holidaymakers sunning themselves on a sward of green paper grass laid out in front of their trailer. He could reproduce the whole screenplay of old movies or daytime radio serials, twisting them here and there with touches of nutty invention— the Lone Ranger as a fag. And mad Catholic fantasies too—Christ at St. Patrick's Cathedral:

"Don't look now, but you'll never guess who's in tonight."

"Which one, which one?"

"The one that's glowing, dummy."

"Police! You've got to get me out of here. I'm up to my ass in wheel chairs and crutches."

Or an M.C.A. agent on the line to Pope John—"Sure we can get you the Sullivan show. But wear the big ring, Johnny. No. No one'll guess you're Jewish."

He did not actually create all this stuff on the stage as he went along. Anyone who saw him regularly began to realize that he had a vast repertoire of "bits" and that the improvisation consisted in the unexpected way he would weave it all together, sometimes only alluding to sketches which he might have played in full the night before.

This would often madden people who only managed to see him once or twice. But it was an indication of the affectionate trust he had in his audience. Without any arrogance, he expected people to come again and again, to join him in creating the rambling, show-biz-saturated saga of American life. He was not a conventional night-club comic who could be guaranteed to deliver a self-contained package of laughing matter for a casual door trade. But like an old-time story teller he was always filling out familiar routines with unexpected additions of vivid new detail. It was impossible to judge him fairly on a single showing. It's a shame that we'll never have a chance of arriving at a just summary. Because apart from a few rather meager and slightly inaudible records, his creation dies with him. Unlike his conventional colleagues, most of whom held him in contempt, he was quite unfitted for mechanical reproduction, since his art and his personality were indistinguishable.

He came to London during the summer of 1961 and I met him for the first time about ten days before he was due to open. He was upstairs in the office of The Establishment, seated on the edge of a desk, bent over an electrical gadget which he was trying to fix with a bread knife. He had obviously been engaged in this for some time because a secretary was twiddling her thumbs at another desk, plainly rather at a loss. He was dressed in a black uniform with a high Nehru collar, open to show an orange T shirt. On his feet he had what looked like high-heeled white cricket boots. The secretary introduced me tentatively, and Bruce looked up, sweating from the exertion of his obscure task. "Hiya Jonathan. Hey, yah." He breathed with vague unfocused enthusiasm. And then he caught sight of a motorcycle helmet I was holding. "Hey man, what do you ride?" "A motor scooter," I said apologetically. After which it took nearly ten days to regain his interest and confidence. But then he never really displayed anything one could call direct personal interest. It was just a restless, incoherent curiosity which he would try to satisfy by quizzing more or less anyone with whom he came in contact. And he was always off at odd tangents—worrying about some gadget, or else running on about a doctor he had heard of who could get him prescriptions. Then there was endless trouble about his hotel accommodation. Largely because of girls, but also because hotel proprietors were badly jangled by his eccentric diurnal routines. Not that he was a night person, or anything straight-forwardly hippy like that. He followed no discernible rhythm whatever in his sleeping and waking. He might sleep for twenty-four hours, and then race around for another forty-eight, walking the streets of Soho, taking down notes about clothes in shop windows, or stopping passers-by to ask them about their jobs. Sometimes he would cat-nap in the office while the secretaries clattered on all round him. And as the opening drew nearer he became more and more noncommittal about what he was actually going to do on the stage; though he would spend hours panting and squawking over a grubby screed to which he kept adding and then crossing out. Or out of the blue he would dictate some dubious paragraph to one of the bewildered girls in the office who had by this time developed a distracted affection for the man. Then he held a press conference and baffled all the reporters, who had expected to find a ferocious slavering junkie, by mildly asking them so many questions about themselves that they never seemed able to get one in edgeways about him. He was always intrigued by their cameras and anyone unlucky enough to be sporting an unusual model had to suffer endless catechism while Bruce turned the machine over lovingly in his hands, breathing and crooning with a naïve, savage wonder. Bruce had plenty of "character" but seemed to possess nothing that one could properly call a personality. There were so many epicycles of interest and activity that it was impossible to make out the central point around which they all moved. Perhaps there wasn't any. I often thought of him like Peter Pan, resolutely fickle and somehow in flight from his and everyone else's maturity. He was comparatively young when he died and yet it was hard to imagine him being any older. His special talent arose from a sort of daft, alienated infantilism which ruled out the possibility of his ever enjoying senior citizenship. Perhaps in some obscure vision of expediency he sought the ordeal which brought about his own annihilation. The horrible thing is that in will: his own execution Bruce actually found society only too willing to oblige him with cruel and extravagant fulfilment.

—October 6, 1966

4

ROBERT LOWELL
ON JOHN BERRYMAN

I SIT LOOKING out a window at 3:30 this February afternoon. I see a pasture, green out of season and sunlit; in an hour more or less, it will be black. John Berryman walks brightly out of my memory. We met at Princeton through Caroline Gordon, in 1944, the wane of the war. The moment was troubled; my wife, Jean Stafford, and I were introduced to the Berrymans for youth and diversion. I remember expected, probably false, images, the hospital-white tablecloth, the clear martinis, the green antiquing of an Ivy League college faculty club. What college? Not Princeton, but the less spruce Cambridge, England, John carried with him in his speech rhythms and dress. He had a casual intensity, the almost intimate mumble of a don. For life, he was to be a student, scholar, and teacher. I think he was almost *the* student-friend I've had, the one who was the student in essence. An indignant spirit was born in him; his life was a cruel fight to set it free. Is the word for him courage or generosity or loyalty? He had these. And he was always a performer, a prima donna; at first to those he scorned, later to everyone, except perhaps students, his family, and Saul Bellow.

From the first, John was humorous, learned, thrustingly vehement in liking...more adolescent than boyish. He and I preferred critics who were writers to critics who were not writers. We hated literary discussions animated by jealousy and pushed by caution. John's own criticism, mostly spoken, had a poetry. Hyperenthusiasms made him a hot friend, and could also make him wearing to friends—one of his dearest, Delmore Schwartz, used to say no one had John's loyalty, but you liked him to live in another city. John had fire then, but not the fire of Byron or Yevtushenko. He clung so keenly to Hopkins, Yeats, and Auden that their shadows paled him.

Later, the Berrymans (the first Berrymans, the first Lowells) stayed with us in Damariscotta Mills, Maine. Too many guests had accepted. We were inept and uncouth at getting the most out of the country; we didn't own or drive a car. This gloomed and needled the guests. John was ease and light. We gossiped on the rocks of the mill-pond, baked things in shells on the sand, and drank, as was the appetite of our age, much less than now. John could quote with vibrance to all lengths, even prose, even late Shakespeare, to show me what could be done with disrupted and mended syntax. This was the start of his real style. At first he wrote with great brio bristles of clauses, all breaks and with little to break off from. Someone said this style was like Emily Dickinson's mad dash punctuation without the words. I copied, and arrived at a manner that made even the verses I wrote for my cousins' *bouts rimés* (with "floor," "door," "whore," and "more" for the fixed rhymes) leaden and unintelligible. Nets so grandly knotted could only catch logs—our first harsh, inarticulate cry of truth.

My pilgrimage to Princeton with Randall Jarrell to have dinner with the Berrymans was not happy. Compared with other poets John was a prodigy; compared with Randall, a slow starter. Perpetrators of such mis-encounters usually confess their bewilderment that two talents with so much in common failed to jell. So much in common—both were slightly heretical disciples of Bernard Haggin, the music and record critic. But John jarred the evening by playing his own favorite recordings on an immense machine constructed and formerly used by Haggin. This didn't animate things; they tried ballet. One liked Covent Garden, the other Danilova, Markova, and the latest New York Balanchine. Berryman unfolded leather photograph books of enlarged British ballerinas he had almost dated. Jarrell made cool, odd evaluations drawn from his forty, recent, consecutive nights of New York ballet. He hinted that the English dancers he had never seen were on a level with the Danes. I suffered more than the fighters, and lost authority by trying not to take sides.

Both poet-critics had just written definitive essay-reviews of my first book, *Lord Weary's Castle*. To a myopic eye, they seemed to harmonize. So much the worse. Truth is in minute particulars; here, in the minutiae, nothing meshed. Earlier in the night, Berryman made the tactical mistake of complimenting Jarrell on his essay. This was accepted with a hurt, glib croak, "Oh thanks." The flattery was not returned, not a muscle smiled. I realized that if the essays were to be written again.... On the horrible New Jersey midnight local to Pennsylvania Station, Randall analyzed John's high, intense voice with surprise and coldness. "Why hasn't anyone told him?" Randall had the same high, keyed-up voice he criticized. Soon he developed chills and fevers, ever more violent, and I took my suit-coat and covered him. He might have been a child. John, the host, the insulted one, recovered sooner. His admiration for Randall remained unsoured, but the dinner was never repeated.

Our trip a year later to Ezra Pound at St. Elizabeth's Hospital near Washington was softer, so soft I remember nothing except a surely misplaced image of John sitting on the floor hugging his knees, and asking with shining cheeks for Pound to sing an aria from his opera *Villon*. He saw nothing nutty about Pound, or maybe it was the opposite. Anyway his instincts were true—serene, ungrudging, buoyant.

Few people, even modern poets, felt carefree and happy with Pound then....When we came back to my room, I made the mistake of thinking that John was less interested in his new poems than in mine.... Another opera. Much later, in the ragged days of John's first divorce, we went to the Met Opera Club, and had to borrow Robert Giroux's dinner jacket and tails. I lost the toss and wore the tails. I see John dancing in the street shouting, "I don't know you, Elizabeth wouldn't know you, only your mother would."

Pound, Jarrell, and Berryman had the same marvelous and maddening characteristic: they were self-centered and unselfish. This gave that breathless, commanding rush to their amusements and controversies—to Jarrell's cool and glowing critical appreciations, to Berryman's quotations and gossip. His taste for what he despised was infallible; but he could outrageously hero worship living and dead, most of all writers his own age. Few have died without his defiant, heroic dirge. I think he sees them rise from their graves like soldiers to answer him.

Jarrell's death was the sadder. If it hadn't happened, it wouldn't have happened. He would be with me now, in full power, as far as one may at fifty. This might-have-been (it's a frequent thought) stings my eyes. John, with pain and joy like his friend Dylan Thomas, almost won what he gambled for. He was more eccentric than Thomas, less the natural poet of natural force, yet had less need to be first actor. He grew older, drier, more toughly twisted into the varieties of experience.

I must say something of death and the *extremist poets*, as we are named in often prefunerary tributes. Except for Weldon Kees and Sylvia Plath, they lived as long as Shakespeare, outlived Wyatt, Baudelaire, and Hopkins, and long outlived the forever Romantics, those who really died young. John himself lived to the age of Beethoven, whom he celebrates in the most ambitious and perhaps finest of his late poems, a monument to his long love, unhampered expression, and subtle criticism. John died with fewer infirmities than Beethoven. The consolation somehow doesn't wash. I feel the jagged gash with which my contemporaries died, with which we were to die. Were they killed, as standard radicals say, by our corrupted society? Was their success an aspect of their destruction? Were we uncomfortable epigoni of Frost, Pound, Eliot, Marianne Moore, etc.? This bitter possibility came to us at the moment of our *arrival*. Death comes sooner or later, these made it sooner.

I somehow smile, though a bit crookedly, when I think of John's whole life, and even of the icy leap from the bridge to the hard ground. He was springy to the end, and on his feet. The cost of his career is shown by an anecdote he tells in one of the earlier *Dream Songs*—as a boy the sliding seat in his shell slipped as he was rowing a race, and he had to push back and forth bleeding his bottom on the runners, till the race was finished. The bravery is ignominious and screams. John kept rowing; maybe at the dock no one noticed the blood on his shorts—his injury wasn't maiming. Going to one of his later Minnesota classes, he stumbled down the corridor, unhelped, though steadying himself step by step on the wall, then taught his allotted hour, and walked to the ambulance he had ordered certain he would die of a stroke while teaching. He was sick a few weeks, then returned to his old courses—as good as before.

The brighter side is in his hilarious, mocking stories, times with wives, children, and friends, and surely in some of the sprinted affairs he fabled. As he became more inspired and famous and drunk, more and more John Berryman, he became less good company and more a happening—slashing eloquence in undertones, amber tumblers of Bourbon, a stony pyramid talking down a rugful of admirers. His almost inhuman generosity sweetened this, but as the heart grew larger, the hide grew thicker. Is his work worth it to us? Of course; though the life of the ant is more to the ant than the health of his anthill. He never stopped fighting and moving all his life; at first, expert and derivative, later the full output, more juice, more pages, more strange words on the page, more simplicity, more obscurity. I am afraid I mistook it for forcing, when he came into his own. No voice now or persona sticks in my ear as his. It is poignant, abrasive, anguished, humorous. A voice on the page, identifiable as my friend's on the telephone, though lost now to mimicry. We should hear him read aloud. It is we who are labored and private, when he is smiling.

I met John last a year or so ago at Christmas in New York. He had been phoning poems and invitations to people at three in the morning, and I felt a weariness about seeing him. Since he had let me sleep uncalled, I guessed he felt numbness to me. We met one noon during the taxi strike at the Chelsea Hotel, dusty with donated, avant-garde constructs, and dismal with personal recollections, Bohemia, and the death of Thomas. There was no cheerful restaurant within walking distance, and the seven best bad ones were closed. We settled for the huge, varnished unwelcome of an empty cafeteria-bar. John addressed me with an awareness of his dignity, as if he were Ezra Pound at St. Elizabeth's, emphatic without pertinence, then brownly inaudible.

His remarks seemed guarded, then softened into sounds that only he could understand or hear. At first John was ascetically hung over, at the end we were high without assurance, and speechless. I said, "When will I see you again?" meaning, in the next few days before I flew to England. John said, "Cal, I was thinking through lunch that I'll never see you again." I wondered how in the murk of our conversation I had hurt him, but he explained that his doctor had told him one more drunken binge would kill him. Choice? It is blighting to know that this fear was the beginning of eleven months of abstinence...half a year of prolific rebirth, then suicide.

I have written on most of Berryman's earlier books. *77 Dream Songs* are harder than most hard modern poetry, the succeeding poems in *His Toy* are as direct as a prose journal, as readable as poetry can be. This is a fulfillment, yet the *77 Songs* may speak clearest, almost John's whole truth. I misjudged them, and was rattled by their mannerisms. His last two books, *Love & Fame* and *Delusions, etc.*, move. They may be slighter than the chronicle of dream songs, but they fill out the frame, alter their speech with age, and prepare for his death—they almost bury John's love-child and ventriloquist's doll, Henry. *Love & Fame* is profane and often in bad taste, the license of John's old college dates recollected at fifty. The subjects may have been too inspiring and less a breaking of new ground than he knew; some wear his gayest cloth. *Love & Fame* ends with an intense long prayer sequence. *Delusions* is mostly sacred and begins with a prayer sequence.

Was riot or prayer delusion? Both were tried friends. The prayers are a Roman Catholic unbeliever's, seesawing from sin to piety, from blasphemous affirmation to devoted anguish. Their trouble is not the dark Hopkins discovered in himself and invented. This is a traditionally Catholic situation, the *Sagesse*, the wisdom of the sinner, Verlaine in jail. Berryman became one of the few religious poets, yet it isn't my favorite side, and I will end with two personal quotations. The first is humorous, a shadow portrait:

> *... My marvelous black new brim-rolled felt*
> *is both stuffy and raffish.*
> *I hit my summit with it, in firelight.*
> *Maybe I only got a Yuletide tie*
> *(increasing sixty) & some writing paper*
> *but ha(haha) I've bought myself a hat!*
> *Plus strokes from position zero!*

The second is soberly prophetic and goes back twenty-six years to when John was visiting Richard Blackmur a few days before or after he visited me:

Understanding
He was reading late, at Richard's down in Maine,
aged 32? Richard and Helen long in bed,
my good wife long in bed.
All I had to do was strip & get in my bed,
putting the marker in the book, and sleep,
& wake to a hot breakfast.

Off the coast was an island, P'tit Manaan,
the bluff from Richard's lawn was almost sheer.
A chill at four o'clock.
It only takes a few minutes to make a man.
A concentration upon now and here.
Suddenly, unlike Bach,

& horribly, unlike Bach, it occurred to me
that one night instead of warm pajamas,
I'd take off all my clothes
& cross the damp cold lawn & totter down the bluff
into the terrible water & walk forever
under it out toward the island.

—April 6, 1972

5

STEPHEN SPENDER
ON W.H. AUDEN

This is the address which Mr. Spender gave at the Cathedral Church, Oxford, on October 27, 1973, in memory of W.H. Auden.

THIS GATHERING OF friends to honor and remember Wystan Auden is not an occasion on which I should attempt to discuss either Wystan's personality or his place in the history of English literature. It is, rather, one on which to recall his presence, and express our praise and gratitude for his life and work, in these surroundings where, intellectually and as a poet, his life may be said to have come full circle.

He was a citizen of the world, a New Yorker with a home in Austria, in the little village of Kirchstetten, where he is buried, for whom Christ Church, "The House," had come to mean his return to his English origins. For making this possible, the Dean and Canon and students are to be thanked.

I knew Wystan since the time when we were both undergraduates, and saw him at intervals until a few weeks before his death. It is impossible for me, in these surroundings, not to juxtapose two images of him, one of forty years back, and one of a year ago only.

The first is of the tow-haired undergraduate poet with the abruptly turning head, and eyes that could quickly take the measure of people or ideas. At that time, he was not altogether quite un-chic, wearing a bow-tie and on occasion wishing one to admire the suit he had on. He recited poetry by heart in an almost toneless, unemotional, quite unpoetical voice which submerged the intellectual meaning under the level horizontal line of the words. He could hold up a word or phrase like an isolated fragment or specimen chipped off the great granite cliff of language, where a tragic emotion could be compressed into a coldly joking word, as in certain phrases I recall him saying. For instance:

The icy precepts of respect

or

Pain has an element of blank

or perhaps lines of his own just written:

Tonight when a full storm surrounds the house
And the fire creaks, the many come to mind
Sent forward in the thaw with anxious marrow.
For such might now return with a bleak face,
An image pause, half-lighted at the door....

A voice, really, in which he could insulate any two words so that they seemed separate from the rest of the created universe, and sent a freezing joking thrill down one's spine. For instance, the voice in which, one summer when he was staying with me at my home in London during a heat wave, and luncheon was served and the dish cover lifted, he exclaimed in tones of utter condemnation like those of a judge passing a terrible sentence:

"Boiled ham!"

The second image of Wystan is of course one with which you are all familiar: the famous poet with the face like a map of physical geography, criss-crossed and river-run and creased with lines. This was a face upon which experiences and thoughts had hammered; a face of isolated self-communing which reminded me of a phrase of Montherlant's about the artist's task of "noble self-cultivation"; a face, though, which was still somehow entertaining and which could break down into a smile of benevolence or light up with gratified recognition at some anecdote recounted or thought received. It was a face at once armored and receptive.

It is difficult to bring these two images—spaced forty years apart—together. But to do so is to find reason for our being here to praise and thank him.

His fellow undergraduates who were poets when he was also an undergraduate (Day Lewis, MacNeice, Rex Warner, and myself) saw in him a man who, instead of being, like us, romantically confused, diagnosed the condition of contemporary poetry, and of civilization, and of us—with our neuroses. He found symptoms everywhere. *Symptomatic* was his key word. But in his very strange poetry he transmogrified these symptoms into figures in a landscape of mountains, passes, streams, heroes, horses, eagles, feuds and runes of Norse sagas. He was a poet of an unanticipated kind—a different race from ourselves—and also a diagnostician of literary, social, and individual psychosomatic situations, who mixed this Iceland imagery with Freudian dream symbolism. Not in the least a leader, but, rather, a clinical-minded oracle with a voice that could sound as depersonalized as a Norn's in a Norse saga. Extremely funny, and extremely hardworking: always, as Louis MacNeice put it, "getting on with the job." He could indulge in self-caricature, and he could decidedly shock, but he did no imitations of other people's speech or mannerisms, though he could do an excellent performance of a High Mass, including the bell tinkling. His only performance was himself.

He was in no sense public and he never wanted to start any kind of literary movement, issue any manifestoes. He was publicly private.

Private faces in public places
Are wiser and nicer
Than public faces in private places.

We were grateful for a person who was so different from ourselves, not quite a person in the way that other people were. His poetry was unlike anything we had expected poetry to be, from our public-school-classical-Platonic-Romantic Eng. Lit. education at that time.

He seemed the incarnation of a serious joke. Wystan wrote somewhere that a friend is simply someone of whom, in his absence, one thinks with pleasure. When Wystan was not there, we spoke of him not only with pleasure and a certain awe, but also laughing. People sometimes divide others into those you laugh at and those you laugh with. The young Auden was someone you could laugh-at-with.

I should say that for most of his friends who were his immediate contemporaries, the pattern of his relationship with them was that of colleague; with his pupils that of a teacher whom they called "Uncle Wiz." During the years when he was teaching at prep school, he wrote his happiest poetry. But in those days of exuberance, merging into the vociferous and partisan 1930s, he almost became that figurehead concerning whose pronouncements he grew to be so self-critical later on: the voice of his generation. Or, rather, its several voices, under which his own voice sometimes seemed muted. For it was not true to his own voice to make public political noises. His own voice said:

O love, the interest itself in thoughtless Heaven,
Make simpler daily the beating of man's heart.

Nevertheless he did speak for the liveliest of the young at that time: those who wanted to throw off the private inhibitions and the public acquiescences of a decade of censorship and dictatorship and connivance with dictatorship, those who were impassioned by freedom, and some who fought for it. He gave to them their wishes which they might not have listened to otherwise. They were grateful for that. He enabled impulses to flower in individuals. All that was life-enhancing.

Thinking now of the other face, of the later Auden, a great many things about him, quite apart from his appearance, had changed. He now mistrusted his past impulsiveness and rejected in his *oeuvre* many lines and stanzas which had been the results of it. His buffoonery was now sharpened and objectified into wit. His eccentricities had rigidified into habits imposed according to a built-in timetable regulating nearly every hour of his day. This was serious but at the same time savingly comic. He never became respectable, could always be outrageous, and occasionally undermined his own interests by giving indiscreet interviews about his life. These tended to disqualify him in the eyes of members of committees dedicated to maintaining respectability.

He had also perhaps acquired some tragic quality of isolation. But with him the line of tragedy coincided almost with that of comedy. That was grace. One reason for this was his total lack of self-pity. He was grateful that he was who he was, namely W. H. Auden, received on earth as an honored guest. His wonderfully positive gratitude for his own good luck prevented him from ever feeling in the least sorry for himself. Audiences were baffled and enchanted by this publicly appearing very private performer, serious and subtle and self-parodying all at the same time. They could take him personally and seriously, laughing at-with-him.

He had become a Christian. There was a side to this conversion which contributed to his personal isolation. Going to Spain because he sympathized with the Republic during the Spanish Civil War, he was nevertheless—and much to his own surprise—shocked at the gutted desolation of burned-out churches. Later, he had some signal visionary experiences. These he did not discuss. He was altered in his relations with people, withdrawn into his own world which included our world, became one of those whom others stare at, from the outside.

In his poetry Christianity appears as a literally believed in mythical interpretation of life which reveals more truth about human nature than that provided by "the healers at the end of city drives" —Freud, Groddeck, Homer Lane, Schweitzer, Nansen, Lawrence, Proust, Kafka—whom Auden had celebrated in his early work as those who had "unlearned hatred,"

and towards the really better
World had turned their face.

For throughout the whole development of his poetry (if one makes exception of the undergraduate work) his theme had been love: not Romantic love but love as interpreter of the world, love as individual need, and love as redeeming power in the life of society and of the individual. At first there was the Lawrentian idea of unrepressed sexual fulfillment through love; then that of the social revolution which would accomplish the change of heart that would change society; then, finally, Christianity which looked more deeply into the heart than any of these, offered man the chance of redeeming himself and the society, but also without illusions showed him to himself as he really was with all the limitations of his nature. Christianity changed not only Auden's ideas but also in some respects his personality. Good qualities which he had always had, of kindness and magnanimity, now became principles of living; not principles carried out on principle, but as realizations of his deepest nature, just as prayer corresponded to his deepest need.

Of all my friends, Wystan was the best at saying "No." But if asked for bread, he never produced a stone. Young poets who brought him their poems were told what he thought about them. (Though, in their case, if he gave them a discourse on prosody, they may have thought that, instead of bread, he was giving them a currant bun.) He no longer believed in the efficacy of any political action a poet might undertake: but that did not mean he had no social conscience. A few years ago I told him that some writers in Budapest had said to me that if he would attend a conference of their local PEN club which was soon to take place, the name Auden would impress the authorities, and their lives perhaps become a bit easier. Wystan left Vienna almost immediately and attended their meeting in Budapest.

Still, he no longer believed that anything a poet writes can influence or change the public world. All a poet can do perhaps is create verbal models of the private life; a garden where people can cultivate an imagined order like that which exists irresistibly in the music of Mozart, and perhaps really, within eternity.

Much of his later poetry was a long retreat from his earlier belief in the feasibility of healing literature, into the impregnable earthworks and fortresses of language itself, the fourteen-volume Oxford dictionary, the enchanted plots of poetic forms in George Saintsbury's book on English prosody, the liquid architecture of Mozart, and the solitaire of *The Times* crossword puzzles.

* * *

Wystan died a month ago now. How long ago it seems. In the course of these few weeks much has happened which makes me feel he may be glad to be rid of this world. One of his most persistent ideas was that one's physical disorders are reflections of the state of one's psyche, expressing itself in a psychosomatic language of spots and coughs and cancers, unconsciously able to choose, I suppose, when to live and when to die. So I am hardly being superstitious in joking with him beyond the grave with the idea that his wise unconscious self chose a good day for dying, just before the most recent cacophonies of political jargon blaring destruction, which destroy the delicate reduced and human scale of language in which individuals are able to communicate in a civilized way with one another.

We can be grateful for the intricate, complex, hand-made engines of language he produced, like the small-scale machinery he so loved of Yorkshire mines, or like the limestone landscapes of that Northern countryside of hills and caves and freshets where he spent his childhood. He made a world of his imagination and had absorbed into his inner life our outer world, which he made accessible to us in his poetry as forms and emblems to play with. His own inner world included his friends, whom he thought about constantly.

He also had a relationship, which one can only describe as one of affection, with an audience, wherever that happened to be. He could project the private reality of his extraordinary presence and voice onto a public platform when he gave a public reading. He provoked some uniquely personal reaction from each member of his audience, as though his presence had dissolved it into all its individual human components.

The last time we met in America I asked him how a reading which he had given in Milwaukee had gone. His face lit up with a smile that altered its lines, and he said: "They loved me!" At first I was surprised at this expression of unabashed pleasure in a public occasion. Then I thought, how right of him. For he had turned the public occasion into everyone's private triumph. One reason why he liked writing—

and reciting—his poetry was that a poem is written by one person writing for one person reading or listening—however many readers or listeners there may be. So as a public, an audience, a meeting of his friends as separate individuals here gathered together, may each of us think separately our gratitude for his fulfilled life and our praise for his completed work.

—November 29, 1973

6

MARY MCCARTHY
ON HANNAH ARENDT

I DO NOT want to discuss Hannah's ideas here but to try to bring her back as a person, a physical being, showing herself radiantly in what she called the world of appearance, a stage from which she has now withdrawn. She was a beautiful woman, alluring, seductive, feminine, which is why I said "Jewess"—the old-fashioned term, evoking the daughters of Sion, suits her, like a fringed Spanish shawl. Above all, her eyes, so brilliant and sparkling, starry when she was happy or excited, but also deep, dark, remote, pools of inwardness. There was something unfathomable in Hannah that seemed to lie in the reflective depths of those eyes.

She had small, fine hands, charming ankles, elegant feet. She liked shoes; in all the years I knew her, I think she only once had a corn. Her legs, feet, and ankles expressed quickness, decision. You had only to see her on a lecture stage to be struck by those feet, calves, and ankles that seemed to keep pace with her thought. As she talked, she moved about, sometimes with her hands plunged in her pockets like somebody all alone on a walk, meditating. When the fire laws permitted, she would smoke, pacing the stage with a cigarette in a short holder, inhaling from time to time, reflectively, her head back, as if arrested by a new, unexpected idea. Watching her talk to an audience was like seeing the motions of the mind made visible in action and gesture. Peripatetic, she would come abruptly to a halt at the lectern, frown, consult the ceiling, bite her lip, pensively cup her chin. If she was reading a speech, there were always interjections, asides, like the footnotes that peppered her texts with qualifications and appendices.

There was more than a touch of the great actress in Hannah. The first time I heard her speak in public—nearly thirty years ago, during a debate—I was reminded of what Bernhardt must have been or Proust's Berma, a magnificent stage diva, which implies a goddess. Perhaps a chthonic goddess, or a fiery one, rather than the airy kind. Unlike other good speakers, she was not at all an orator. She appeared, rather, as a mime, a thespian, enacting a drama of mind, that dialogue of me-and-myself she so often summons up in her writings. Watching her framed in the proscenium arch, we were not far from the sacred origins of the theater. What she projected was the human figure as actor and sufferer in the agon of consciousness and reflection, where there are always two, the one who says and the one who replies or questions.

Yet nobody could have been farther from an exhibitionist. Calculation of the impression she was making never entered her head. Whenever she spoke in public, she had terrible stage fright, and afterward she would ask only "Was it all right?" (This cannot have been true of the classroom, where she felt herself at ease and among friends.) And naturally she did not play roles in private or public, even less than the normal amount required in social relations. She was incapable of feigning. Though she prided herself as a European on being able to tell a lie, where we awkward Americans blurted out the truth, in fact there was a little hubris there. Hannah's small points of vanity never had any relation to her real accomplishments. For example, she thought she knew a good deal about cooking and didn't.

It was the same with her supposed ability to lie. Throughout our friendship, I don't think I ever heard her tell even one of those white lies, such as pleading illness or a previous engagement, to get herself out of a social quandary. If you wrote something she found bad, her policy was not to allude to it—an unvarying course of action that told you louder than words what she thought.

What was theatrical in Hannah was a kind of spontaneous power of being seized by an idea, an emotion, a presentiment, whose vehicle her body then became, like the actor's. And this power of being seized and worked upon, often with a start, widened eyes, "Ach!" (before a picture, a work of architecture, some deed of infamy), set her apart from the rest of us like a high electrical charge. And there was the vibrant, springy, dark, short hair, never fully gray, that sometimes from sheer force of energy appeared to stand bolt upright on her head.

I suppose all this must have been part of an unusual physical endowment, whose manifestation in her features and facial gestures was the beauty I spoke of. Hannah is the only person I have ever watched *think*. She lay motionless on a sofa or a day bed, arms folded behind her head, eyes shut but occasionally opening to stare upward. This lasted—I don't know—from ten minutes to half an hour. Everyone tiptoed past if we had to come into the room in which she lay oblivious.

She was an impatient, generous woman, and those qualities went hand in hand. Just as, in a speech or an essay, she would put everything in but the kitchen stove, as if she could not keep in reserve a single item of what she knew or had happened that instant to occur to her, so she would press on a visitor assorted nuts, chocolates, candied ginger, tea, coffee, Campari, whiskey, cigarettes, cake, crackers, fruit, cheese, almost all at once, regardless of conventional sequence or, often, of the time of day. It was as if the profusion of edibles, set out, many of them, in little ceremonial-like dishes and containers, were impatient propitiatory offerings to all the queer gods of taste. Someone said that this was the eternal Jewish mother, but it was not that: there was no notion that any of this fodder was good for you; in fact most of it was distinctly bad for you, which she must have known somehow, for she did not insist.

She had a respect for privacy, separateness, one's own and hers. I often stayed with her—and Heinrich and her—on Riverside Drive and before that on Morningside Drive, so that I came to know Hannah's habits well, what she liked for breakfast, for instance. A boiled egg, some mornings, a little ham or cold cuts, toast spread with anchovy paste, coffee, of course, half a grapefruit or fresh orange juice, but perhaps that last was only when I, the American, was there. The summer after Heinrich's death she came to stay with us in Maine, where we gave her a separate apartment, over the garage, and I put some thought into buying supplies for her kitchen—she liked to breakfast alone. The things, I thought, that she would have at home, down to instant coffee (which I don't normally stock) for when she could not be bothered with the filters. I was rather pleased to have been able to find anchovy paste in the village store. On the afternoon of her arrival, as I showed her where everything was in the larder, she frowned over the little tube of anchovy paste, as though it were an inexplicable foreign object. "What is that?" I told her. "Oh." She put it down and looked thoughtful and as though displeased, somehow. No more was said. But I knew I had done something wrong in my efforts to please. She did not wish to be *known*, in that curiously finite and, as it were, reductive way. And I had done it to show her I knew her—a sign of love, though not always—thereby proving that in the last analysis I did not know her at all.

Her eyes were closed in her coffin, and her hair was waved back from her forehead, whereas *she* pulled it forward, sometimes tugging at a lock as she spoke, partly to hide a scar she had got in an automobile accident—but even before that she had never really bared her brow. In her coffin, with the lids veiling the fathomless eyes, that noble forehead topped by a sort of pompadour, she was not Hannah any more but a composed death mask of an eighteenth-century philosopher. I was not moved to touch that grand stranger in the funeral parlor, and only in the soft yet roughened furrows of her neck, in which the public head rested, could I find a place to tell her good-by.

—January 22, 1976

7

JOHN THOMPSON
ON ROBERT LOWELL

FORTY YEARS AGO in the carpenter's Gothic of Douglass House, demolished now, at Gambier, Ohio, in the long gabled upstairs room he shared with Peter Taylor, Robert Lowell had the intelligent habit of lying in bed all day. Around that bed like a tumble-down brick wall were his Greek Homer, his Latin Vergil, his Chaucer, letters from Boston, cast-off socks, his Dante, his Milton. Even in those days before he had published a word we knew he belonged among the peers who surrounded him.

The poems he wrote and rewrote and rewrote in bed then were as awkward as he was, the man of the Kenyon squad who plowed sideways into his own teammates, but strong as a bull, spilling them all over, who never won a game. He aspired to be a Rhodes Scholar, and thus had to be an all-around man like Whizzer White. In those days Lowell couldn't tie his own shoe laces.

To our astonishment this nearly inarticulate fellow entered the Ohio state oratory contest. But we were not surprised at all when like Demosthenes he won the prize.

Lowell has written about his mother Charlotte and his father the Naval Commander. Charlotte was a Snow Queen who flirted coldly and shamelessly with her son. His father once ordered a half-bottle of wine for five at dinner.

Lowell brought Jean Stafford to Kenyon, shining she was, wearing a hat and gloves, tucked under her arm a mint copy from England of something mysterious to us, *Goodbye to Berlin*! They married, and, new Catholics, after a year on the *Southern Review* under Brooks and Warren, they holed up in Maine, as both have written. He went to jail as an objector to the War after attempts to get in the Navy. He didn't like it that we had started bombing cities.

* * *

He lived in a fleabag under the old Third Avenue El on about a dollar a day. In the room next door dwelled an ardent couple. "Be quiet," one of them whispered, "the kid there might hear us." He read all the books, and wrote and rewrote his poems. History was his eye-opener and his nightcap. He recited Vergil with Robert Fitzgerald. When he came to supper he ate enough for three days, and then graciously said, "I'm stuffed." He got the Pulitzer Prize.

He went crazy, and being brought toward home after a cross-country charge he squatted, powerful and sweating, in the rotunda that was then LaGuardia airport. The cops came and sat down on the floor with him. They discussed Italian opera. He was taken to the first asylum. Cured, well-known now, he kept writing his wonderful poems. He married Elizabeth Hardwick who brought him up. She gave him Harriet his daughter.

They moved from Boston to New York. Many times Elizabeth, as if Alcestis had had to do it over and over, faced the kingdom of the mad and dragged him home alive. He wrote frankly about his illness. This did not mean he thought it a distinction. He hated it, hated making a fool of himself and being a trouble to other people, hated the time and work lost to it. Everything the doctors prescribed he did but the illness had its own power of accessions and remissions.

Some Lowell money and his own solid earnings brought him and his family a living in fair style. The elegance, grace, and power of a great man came to him without his noticing.

He was big, well-shouldered, and light on his feet but bore a noticeable physical diffidence like a polite stammer. His face was big, gnathic, and classically formed, with owl spectacles that slid down his nose, and his head was feathered around later with his longish gray hair. His fingers were clean and delicate. He poked and pointed with them as he talked. Teasing or telling stories, for instance his endless saga of the tribe of bears whose misbehaviors parodied those of his friends and relations, he had a special sing-song voice. Otherwise, except in public reading, it was a Boston soar then mutter. His only sport was trout-fishing.

He had confounded his old mentors with *Life Studies*, which they said was not literature, and he should not publish. They were right, it was not literature. Blake and Whitman and the man he oddly admired so much, Hart Crane, were not literature either but they made literature move over for them.

Calligraphers recognize in one another's lettering what they call a man's "fist," his unchangeable personal style. Lowell's lines might be pentameters of Miltonic elevation,

> *When the whale's viscera go and the roll*
> *Of its corruption overruns this world*
> *Beyond tree-swept Nantucket and Woods Hole*
> *And Martha's Vineyard, Sailor, will your sword*
> *Whistle and fall and sink into the fat?*

Or they might be in the off-hand slang of his middle period,

> *The season's ill—*

We've lost our summer millionaire,
who seemed to leap from an L.L. Bean
catalogue. His nine-knot yawl
was auctioned off to lobstermen.
A red fox stain covers Blue Hill.

Or, characteristically, the lines bring old catch-phrases to a focus so sharp it hurts.

My hopped up husband drops his home disputes,
and hits the streets to cruise for prostitutes,
free-lancing out along the razor's edge.
This screwball might kill his wife, then take the pledge.

The unchanging element of Lowell's poetry was that whatever he was writing about in whichever one of his many styles, the words loomed everywhere as if in some huge magnifying lens of etymology and idiom and sound—and yet were always in the stream of English speech.

Lowell's genius and his grinding labor brought to verse in English not only technical mastery on a scale otherwise scarcely attempted in this century, but then his courage and honesty brought, to crib from myself, "a new generosity and dignity to the whole enterprise of poetry." He was not afraid of mistakes and made plenty of them, or so it seemed to me, in the mulled-over *Notebook*.

As a boy he had studied Napoleon and he liked being famous. Francis Parker, who did the etchings for every one of Lowell's books, says that while he was chained in the special Nazi cells for Dieppe survivors he would sometimes fancy that his school chum Cal Lowell had at last been named Commander of Allied Forces.

Lowell drank and smoked too much as became his generation,

and tolerated around him an incredible number of fools. If he went to an art museum he liked everything, even nineteenth-century steel engravings; or would say one might come to it if one saw them often. He was fond of going to operas too and liked them all. To fellow poets he was cordial, and respectful of their work. But once in a while in a flash it would come out that he had them all precisely ranked and not so very highly either.

Fame, titles, great names attracted him as they do all those who know their souls belong on the upper slopes. He loved maybe five or six people and he loved them all his life. He was also dangerous, as men in his dimensions can be.

In New York, Lowell ruled a writer's roost as he saw fit, and then married Caroline Blackwood. They lived in England. She gave him his son Sheridan. He wrote every day and read everything, was well and ill, off and on. I am told that the kind of heart attack that took him, in a New York taxi on the afternoon of September 12 as he was returning to Elizabeth and Harriet, just all at once puts you to sleep.

"... I gather from your phone calls the summer has had some very hard moments for you. It's miraculous, as you told me about yourself, how often writing takes the ache away, takes time away. You start in the morning, and look up to see the windows darkening. I'm sure anything done steadily, obsessively, eyes closed to everything besides the page, the spot of garden ... makes returning a jolt. The world you've been saved from grasps you roughly. Even sleep and dreams do this. I have no answer. I think the ambition of art, the feeding on one's soul, memory, mind etc. gives a mixture of glory and exhaustion. I think in the end, there is no end, the thread frays rather than is cut, or if it is cut suddenly, it usually hurtingly frays

before being cut. No perfected end, but a lot of meat and drink along the way."
—Robert Lowell *from a letter to Frank Bidart, September 4, 1976*

—October 27, 1977

8

JAMES MERRILL
ON ELIZABETH BISHOP

SHE DISLIKED BEING photographed and usually hated the result. The whitening hair grew thick above a face each year somehow rounder and softer, like a bemused, blue-lidded planet, a touch too large, in any case, for a body that seemed never quite to have reached maturity. In early life the proportions would have been just right. A 1941 snapshot (printed in last winter's Vassar Bulletin) shows her at Key West, with bicycle, in black French beach togs, beaming straight at the camera: a living doll.

The bicycle may have been the same one she pedaled to the local electric company with her monthly bill *and* Charles Olson's, who one season rented her house but felt that "a Poet mustn't be asked to do prosaic things like pay bills." The story was told not at the Poet's expense but rather as fingers are crossed for luck—another of her own instinctive, modest, lifelong impersonations of an ordinary woman, someone who during the day did errands, went to the beach, would perhaps that evening jot a phrase or two inside the nightclub matchbook before returning to the dance floor.

Thus the later glimpses of her playing was it poker? with Neruda in a Mexican hotel, or ping pong with Octavio Paz in Cambridge, or getting Robert Duncan high on grass—"for the first time!"—in San

Francisco, or teaching Frank Bidart the wildflowers in Maine. Why talk *letters* with one's gifted colleagues? They too would want, surely, to put aside work in favor of a new baby to examine, a dinner to shop for and cook, sambas, vignettes: Here's what I heard this afternoon (or saw twenty years ago)—imagine! Poetry was a life both shaped by and distinct from the lived one, like that sleet storm's second tree "of glassy veins" in "Five Flights Up." She was never unwilling to talk about hers, but managed to make it sound agreeably beside the point. As in her "Miracle for Breakfast" she tended to identify not with the magician on his dawn-balcony but with the onlookers huddled and skeptical in the breadline below.

This need for relief from what must have been an at times painful singularity was coupled with "the gift to be simple" under whatever circumstances. Once, after days of chilly drizzle in Ouro Preto, the sun came out and Elizabeth proposed a jaunt to the next town. There would be a handsome church and, better yet, a jail opposite whose murderers and wife-beaters wove the prettiest little bracelets and boxes out of empty cigarette packages, which they sold through the grille. Next a taxi was jouncing through sparkling red-and-green country, downhill, uphill, then, suddenly, *under* a rainbow! Elizabeth said some words in Portuguese, the driver began to shake with laughter. "In the north of Brazil," she explained, "they have this superstition, if you pass underneath a rainbow you change sex." (We were to pass more than once under this one.) On our arrival the prisoners had nothing to show us. They were mourning a comrade dead that week—six or eight men in their cavernous half-basement a narrow trench of water flowed through. They talked with Elizabeth quietly, like an old friend who would understand. It brought to mind that early prose piece where she imagines, with anything but distaste, being confined for life to a small stone cell. Leaving, she gave them a few coins; she had touched another secret base.

In Ouro Preto literary visitors were often a matter of poets from other parts of Brazil—weren't there 15,000 in Belem alone? These would arrive, two or three a week during the "season," to present her with their pamphlets, receiving in turn an inscribed *Complete Poems* from a stack on the floor beside her. The transaction, including coffee, took perhaps a quarter of an hour, at whose end we were once more by ourselves. The room was large, irregular in shape, the high beams painted. Instead of a picture or mirror one white wall framed a neat rectangular excavation: the plaster removed to show timbers lashed together by thongs. This style of construction dated the house before 1740. Across the room burned the cast-iron stove, American, the only one in town. More echoes, this time from "Sestina."

I was her first compatriot to visit in several months. She found it uncanny to be speaking English again. Her other guest, a young Brazilian painter, in town for the summer arts festival and worn out by long teaching hours, merely slept in the house. Late one evening, over Old-Fashioneds by the stove, a too recent sorrow had come to the surface; Elizabeth, uninsistent and articulate, was in tears. The young painter, returning, called out, entered—and stopped short on the threshold. His hostess almost blithely made him at home. Switching to Portuguese, "Don't be upset, José Alberto," I understood her to say, "I'm only crying in English."

The next year, before leaving Brazil for good, she went on a two-week excursion up the Rio Negro. One day the rattletrap white river-steamer was accosted by a wooden melon-rind barely afloat, containing a man, a child of perhaps six, and a battered but ornate armchair which they were hoping to sell. Nothing doing. However, a "famous eye" among the passengers was caught by the boatman's paddle—a splendidly sanded and varnished affair painted with the flags of Brazil and the United States; it would hang on her wall in Boston. When the riverman understood that the eccentric foreign Senhora was offering, for this implement on which his poor livelihood depended, more money ($6, if memory serves) than he could dream of refusing, his perplexity knew no bounds. Then the little boy spoke up: "Sell it Papá, we still have *my* paddle!"—waving one no bigger than a toy. Which in the event, the bargain struck, would slowly, comically, precariously ply them and their unsold throne back across the treacherous water.

Will it serve as momentary emblem of her charm as a woman and her wisdom as a poet? The adult, in charge of the craft, keeping it balanced, richer for a loss; the child coming up with means that, however slow, quirky, humble, would nevertheless—

Nevertheless, with or without emblems, and hard as it is to accept that there will be no more of them, her poems remain. One has to blush, faced with poems some of us feel to be more wryly radiant, more touching, more unaffectedly intelligent than any written in our lifetime, to come up with such few blurred snapshots of their maker. It is not her writings—even to those magically chatty letters—whose loss is my subject here. Those miracles outlast their performer; but for her the sun has set, and for us the balcony is dark.

—December 6, 1979

9

ISAIAH BERLIN
ON BORIS PASTERNAK AND
ANNA AKHMATOVA

I

IN THE SUMMER of 1945 the British Embassy in Moscow reported that it was short-handed, especially in the matter of officials who knew Russian, and it was suggested that I might fill a gap for four or five months. I accepted this offer eagerly, mainly, I must admit, because of my great desire to learn about the condition of Russian literature and art, about which relatively little was known in the West at that time. I knew something, of course, of what had happened to Russian writers and artists in the Twenties and Thirties. The Revolution had stimulated a great wave of creative energy in Russia, in all the arts; bold experimentalism was everywhere encouraged: the new controllers of culture did not interfere with anything that could be represented as being a "slap in the face" to bourgeois taste, whether it was Marxist or not. The new movement in the visual arts—the work of such painters as Kandinsky, Chagall, Soutine, Malevich, Klyun, Tatlin, the sculptors Arkhipenko, Pevsner, Gabo, Lipchitz, Zadkine, of the theater and film directors Meyerhold, Vakhtangov, Tairov, Eisenstein, Pudovkin—produced masterpieces which had a powerful impact in the West; there was a similar upward curve in the field of literature and literary criticism. Despite the violence and devastation of the Civil War, and the ruin and chaos brought about by it, revolutionary art of extraordinary vitality continued to be produced.

I remember meeting Sergei Eisenstein in 1945; he was in a state of terrible depression: this was the result of Stalin's condemnation of the original version of his film *Ivan the Terrible*, because that savage ruler, with whom Stalin identified himself, faced with the need to repress the treachery of the *boyars*, had, so Stalin complained, been misrepresented as a man tormented to the point of neurosis. I asked Eisenstein what he thought were the best years of his life. He answered without hesitation, "The early Twenties. That was the time. We were young and did marvelous things in the theater. I remember once, greased pigs were let loose among the members of the audience, who leaped on their seats and screamed. It was terrific. Goodness, how we enjoyed ourselves!"

This was obviously too good to last. An onslaught was delivered on it by leftist zealots who demanded collective proletarian art. Then Stalin decided to put an end to all these politico-literary squabbles as a sheer waste of energy—not at all what was needed for Five Year Plans. The Writers' Union was created in the mid-Thirties to impose orthodoxy. There was to be no more argument, no disturbance of men's minds. A dead level of conformism followed. Then came the final horror—the Great Purge, the political show trials, the mounting terror of 1937-1938, the wild and indiscriminate mowing down of individuals and groups, later of whole peoples. I need not dwell on the facts of that murderous period, not the first, or probably the last, in the history of Russia. Authentic accounts of the life of the intelligentsia in that time are to be found in the memoirs of, for example, Nadezhda Mandelstam, Lydia Chukovskaya, and, in a different sense, in Akhmatova's poem *Requiem*. In 1939 Stalin called a halt to the proscriptions. Russian literature, art, and thought emerged like an area that had been subjected to bombardment, with some noble buildings still relatively intact, but standing bare and solitary in a landscape of ruined and deserted streets.

Then came the German invasion, and an extraordinary thing happened. The need to achieve national unity in the face of the enemy led to some relaxation of the political controls. In the great wave of Russian patriotic feeling, writers old and young, particularly poets, whom their readers felt to be speaking for them, for what they themselves felt and believed—these writers were idolized as never before. Poets whose work had been regarded with disfavor by the authorities, and consequently published seldom, if at all, suddenly received letters from soldiers at the fronts, as often as not quoting their least political and most personal lines. Boris Pasternak and Anna Akhmatova, who had for a long time lived in a kind of internal exile, began to receive an astonishingly large number of letters from soldiers quoting from both published and unpublished poems; there was a stream of requests for autographs, for confirmation of the authenticity of texts, for expressions of the author's attitude to this or that problem. In the end this impressed itself on the minds of some of the Party's leaders. The status and personal security of these frowned-upon poets were, in consequence, improved. Public readings by poets, as well as the reciting from memory of poetry at private gatherings, had been common in pre-revolutionary Russia. What was novel was that when Pasternak and Akhmatova read their poems, and occasionally halted for a word, there were always, among the vast audiences gathered to hear them, scores of listeners who prompted them at once with lines from works both published and unpublished, and in any case not publicly available. No writer could help being moved and drawing strength from this most genuine form of homage.

The status of the handful of poets who clearly rose far above the rest was, I found, unique. Neither painters nor composers nor prose

writers, not even the most popular actors, or eloquent, patriotic journalists, were loved and admired so deeply and so universally, especially by the kind of people I spoke to in trams and trains and the
subway, some of whom admitted that they had never read a word of
their writings. The most famous and widely worshipped of all Russian poets was Boris Pasternak. I longed to meet him more than any
other human being in the Soviet Union. I was warned that it was very
difficult to meet those whom the authorities did not permit to appear
at official receptions, where foreigners could meet only carefully selected Soviet citizens—the others had had it very forcibly impressed
upon them that it was neither desirable nor safe for them to meet
foreigners, particularly in private. I was lucky. By a fortuitous con-
catenation of circumstances, I did contrive, very early during my
stay, to call upon Pasternak at his country cottage in the writers' village of Peredelkino, near Moscow.

II

I went to see him on a warm, sunlit afternoon in September 1945.
The poet, his wife, and his son Leonid were seated round a rough
wooden table at the back of the *dacha*. Pasternak greeted me warmly.
He was once described by his friend, the poet Marina Tsvetaeva, as
looking like an Arab and his horse—he had a dark, melancholy, ex-
pressive, very *racé* face, familiar from many photographs and from
his father's paintings. He spoke slowly in a low tenor monotone, with
a continuous even sound, something between a humming and a
drone, which those who met him almost always remarked upon: each
vowel was elongated as if in some plaintive aria in an opera by Tchai-
kovsky, but with far more concentrated force and tension.

Almost at once Pasternak said, "You come from England. I was in

London in the Thirties—in 1935, on my way back from the Anti-Fascist Congress in Paris." He then said that during the summer of that year he had suddenly received a telephone call from the authorities, who told him that a congress of writers was in session in Paris and that he was to go to it without delay. He said that he had no suitable clothes—"We will see to that," said the officials. They tried to fit him out in a formal morning coat and striped trousers, a shirt with stiff cuffs and a wing collar, and black patent leather boots, which fitted perfectly. But he was, in the end, allowed to go in ordinary clothes. He was later told that André Malraux, the organizer of the congress, had insisted on getting him invited; Malraux had told the Soviet authorities that although he fully understood their reluctance to do so, yet not to send Pasternak and Babel to Paris might cause unnecessary speculation; they were very well-known Soviet writers, and there were not many such in those days so likely to appeal to European liberals. "You cannot imagine how many celebrities were there," Pasternak said—"Dreiser, Gide, Malraux, Aragon, Auden, Forster, Rosamond Lehmann, and lots of other terribly famous people. I spoke. I said to them 'I understand that this is a meeting of writers to organize resistance to Fascism. I have only one thing to say to you: do not organize. Organization is the death of art. Only personal independence matters. In 1789, 1848, 1917, writers were not organized for or against anything. Do not, I implore you, do not organize.'

"I think they were surprised, but what else could I say? I thought I would get into trouble at home after that, but no one ever said a word to me about it, then or now. Then I went to London and traveled back in one of our boats, and shared a cabin with Shcherbakov, who was then the secretary of the Writers' Union, tremendously influential, and afterwards a member of the Politburo. I talked unceasingly, day and night. He begged me to stop and let him sleep. But I went on and on. Paris and London had awoken me, I could not stop. He begged for mercy but I was relentless. He must have thought me quite deranged: it may be that this helped me afterwards." He meant, I think, that to be thought a little mad, or at least extremely eccentric, may have helped to save him during the Great Purge.

Pasternak then asked me if I had read his prose, in particular *The Childhood of Lüvers*. "I see by your expression," he said, most unjustly, "that you think that these writings are contrived, tortured, self-conscious, horribly modernist—no, no, don't deny it, you do think this, and you are absolutely right. I am ashamed of them—not of my poetry, but of my prose—it was influenced by what was weakest and most muddled in the symbolist movement, fashionable in those years, full of mystical chaos—of course Andrey Bely was a genius—*Petersburg, Kotik Letaev* are full of wonderful things—I know that, you need not tell me—but his influence was fatal—Joyce is another matter—all that I wrote then was obsessed, forced, broken, artifical, no use [*negodno*]; but now I am writing something entirely different: something new, quite new, luminous, elegant, well-proportioned [*stroinoe*], classically pure and simple—what Winckelmann wanted, yes, and Goethe; and this will be my last word, my most important word, to the world. It is, yes, it is what I wish to be remembered by; I shall devote the rest of my life to it."

I cannot vouch for the complete accuracy of all these words, but this is how I remember them. This projected work later became *Doctor Zhivago*. He had by 1945 completed a draft of a few early chapters, which he asked me to read, and send to his sisters in Oxford; I did so, but was not to know about the plan for the entire novel until much later. After that, Pasternak was silent for a while; none of us spoke. He then told us how much he liked Georgia, Georgian writers, Yashvili, Tabidze, and Georgian wine, how well received there he always was. After this he politely asked me about what was going on in the West; did I know Herbert Read and his doctrine of personalism? Here he explained that his belief in personal freedom was derived from Kantian individualism—Blok had misinterpreted Kant completely in his poem *Kant*. There was nothing here in Russia about which he could tell me. I must realize that the clock had stopped in Russia (I noticed that neither he nor any of the other writers I met ever used the words "Soviet Union") in 1928 or so, when relations with the outer world were in effect cut off; the description of him and his work in, for instance, the Soviet Encyclopedia bore no reference to his later life or writings.

He was interrupted by Lydia Seifullina, an elderly, well-known writer, who broke in while he was in mid-course: "My fate is exactly the same," she said: "the last lines of the Encyclopedia article about me say 'Seifullina is at present in a state of psychological and artistic crisis'—the article has not been changed during the last twenty years. So far as the Soviet reader is concerned, I am still in a state of crisis, of suspended animation. We are like people in Pompeii, you and I, Boris Leonidovich, buried by ashes in mid-sentence. And we know so little: Maeterlinck and Kipling, I know, are dead; but Wells, Sinclair Lewis, Joyce, Bunin, Khodasevich—are they alive?" Pasternak looked embarrassed and changed the subject. He had been reading Proust— French communist friends had sent him the entire masterpiece—he knew it, he said, and had reread it lately. He had not then heard of Sartre or Camus, and thought little of Hemingway ("Why Anna Andreevna [Akhmatova] thinks anything of him I cannot imagine," he said).

He spoke in magnificent slow-moving periods, with occasional intense rushes of words. His talk often overflowed the banks of grammatical structure—lucid passages were succeeded by wild but always marvelously vivid and concrete images—and these might be followed by dark words when it was difficult to follow him—and then he would suddenly come into the clear again. His speech was at all times that of a poet, as were his writings. Someone once said that there are poets who are poets when they write poetry and prose-writers when they write prose; others are poets in everything that they write. Pasternak was a poet of genius in all that he did and was. As for his conversation, I cannot begin to describe its quality. The only other person I have met who talked as he talked was Virginia Woolf, who made one's mind race as he did, and obliterated one's normal vision of reality in the same exhilarating and, at times, terrifying way.

I use the word "genius" advisedly. I am sometimes asked what I mean by this highly evocative but imprecise term. In answer I can only say this: the dancer Nijinsky was once asked how he managed to leap so high. He is reported to have answered that he saw no great problem in this. Most people when they leaped in the air came down at once. "Why should you come down immediately? Stay in the air a little before you return, why not?" he is reported to have said. One of the criteria of genius seems to me to be precisely this: the power to do something perfectly simple and visible which ordinary people cannot, and know that they cannot, do—nor do they know how it is done, or why they cannot begin to do it. Pasternak at times spoke in great leaps; his use of words was the most imaginative that I have ever known; it was wild and very moving. There are, no doubt, many varieties of literary genius: Eliot, Joyce, Yeats, Auden, Russell did not (in my experience) talk like this. I did not wish to overstay my welcome. I left the poet, excited, and indeed overwhelmed, by his words and by his personality.

After Pasternak returned to Moscow I visited him almost weekly, and came to know him well. I cannot hope to describe the transforming effect of his presence, his voice and gestures. He talked about books and writers; he loved Proust and was steeped in his writings, and *Ulysses*—he had not, at any rate then, read Joyce's later work.

He spoke about French symbolists, and about Verhaeren and Rilke, both of whom he had met; he greatly admired Rilke, both as a man and a writer. He was steeped in Shakespeare. He was dissatisfied with his own translations: "I have tried to make Shakespeare work for me," he said, "but it has not been a success." He grew up, he said, in the shadow of Tolstoy—for him an incomparable genius, greater than Dickens or Dostoevsky, a writer who stood with Shakespeare and Goethe and Pushkin. His father, the painter, had taken him to see Tolstoy on his deathbed, in 1910, at Astapovo. He found it impossible to be critical towards Tolstoy: Russia and Tolstoy were one. As for Russian poets, Blok was of course the dominant genius of his time, but he did not find him sympathetic. Bely was closer to him, a man of strange and unheard-of insights—magical and a holy fool in the tradition of Russian Orthodoxy. Bryusov he considered a self-constructed, ingenious, mechanical musical-box, a clever, calculating operator, not a poet at all. He did not mention Mandelstam. He felt most tenderly towards Marina Tsvetaeva, to whom he had been bound by many years of friendship.

His feelings towards Mayakovsky were more ambivalent: he had known him well, they had been close friends, and he had learned from him; he was, of course, a titanic destroyer of old forms, but, he added, unlike other communists, he was at all times a human being—but no, not a major poet, not an immortal god like Tyutchev or Blok, not even a demi-god, like Fet or Bely. Time had diminished him. He was needed in his day, he was what those times had called for. There are poets, he said, who have their hour, Aseev, poor Klyuev—liquidated—Sel'vinsky—even Esenin. They fulfill an urgent need of the day, their gifts are of crucial importance to the development of poetry in their country, and then they are no more. Mayakovsky was the greatest of these—*The Cloud in Trousers* had its historical importance, but the shouting was unbearable: he inflated his talent and tortured it until it burst. The sad rags of the multi-colored balloon still lay in one's path, if one was a Russian. He was gifted, important, but coarse and not grown up, and ended as a poster-artist. Mayakovsky's love affairs had been disastrous for him as a man and a poet. He, Pasternak, had loved Mayakovsky as a man; his suicide was one of the blackest days of his own life.

Pasternak was a Russian patriot—his sense of his own historical connection with his country was very deep. He told me, again and again, how glad he was to spend his summers in the writers' village, Peredelkino, for it had once been part of the estate of that great Slavophil, Yury Samarin. The true line of tradition led from the legendary Sadko to the Stroganovs and the Kochubeys, to Derzhavin, Zhukovsky, Tyutchev, Pushkin, Baratynsky, Lermontov, Fet, Annensky, to the Aksakovs, Tolstoy, Bunin—to the Slavophils, not to the liberal intelligentsia, which, as Tolstoy maintained, did not know what men lived by. This passionate, almost obsessive, desire to be thought a true Russian writer, with roots deep in Russian soil, was particularly evident in his negative feelings towards his Jewish origins. He was unwilling to discuss the subject—he was not embarrassed by it, but he disliked it: he wished the Jews to disappear as a people.

His artistic taste had been formed in his youth and he remained faithful to the masters of that period. The memory of Scriabin—he had thought of becoming a composer himself—was sacred to him. I shall not easily forget the paean of praise offered by both Pasternak and Neuhaus (the celebrated musician, and former husband of Pasternak's wife Zinaida) to Scriabin, and to the symbolist painter Vrubel, whom, with Nicholas Roerich, they prized above all contemporary painters. Picasso and Matisse, Braque and Bonnard, Klee and Mondrian, seemed to mean as little to them as Kandinsky or Malevich.

There is a sense in which Akhmatova and her contemporaries Gumilev and Marina Tsvetaeva are the last great voices of the nineteenth century—perhaps Pasternak occupies an interspace between the two centuries, and so, perhaps, does Mandelstam. They were the last representatives of what can only be called the second Russian renaissance, basically untouched by the modern movement, by Picasso, Stravinsky, Eliot, Joyce, Schoenberg, even if they admired them; for the modern movement in Russia was aborted by political events (the poetry of Mandelstam is another story). Pasternak loved Russia. He was prepared to forgive his country all its shortcomings, all, save the barbarism of Stalin's reign; but even that, in 1945, he regarded as the darkness before the dawn which he was straining his eyes to detect—the hope expressed in the last chapters of *Doctor Zhivago*. He believed himself to be in communion with the inner life of the Russian people, to share its hopes and fears and dreams, to be its voice as, in their different fashions, Tyutchev, Tolstoy, Dostoevsky, Chekhov, and Blok had been (by the time I knew him he conceded nothing to Nekrasov).

In conversation with me during my Moscow visits, when we were always alone, before a polished desk on which not a book or a scrap of paper was to be seen, he repeated his conviction that he lived close to the heart of his country, and sternly and repeatedly denied this role of Gorky and Mayakovsky, especially to the former and felt that he had something to say to the rulers of Russia, something of immense importance which only he could say, although what this was—he spoke of it often—seemed dark and incoherent to me. This may well have been due to lack of understanding on my part—although Anna Akhmatova told me that when he spoke in this prophetic strain, she, too, failed to understand him.

It was when he was in one of these ecstatic moods that he told me of his telephone conversation with Stalin about Mandelstam's arrest, the famous conversation of which many differing versions circulated and still circulate. I can only reproduce the story as I remember that he told it me in 1945. According to his account he was in his Moscow flat with his wife and son and no one else when the telephone rang, and a voice told him that it was the Kremlin speaking, and that comrade Stalin wished to speak to him. He assumed that this was an idiotic practical joke, and put down his receiver. The telephone rang again, and the voice somehow convinced him that the call was authentic. Stalin then asked him whether he was speaking to Boris Leonidovich Pasternac. Pasternak said that it was indeed he. Stalin asked whether he was present when a lampoon about himself, Stalin, was recited by Mandelstam. Pasternak answered that it seemed to him of no importance whether he was or was not present, but that he was enormously happy that Stalin was speaking to him; that he had always known that this would happen; that they must meet and speak about matters of supreme importance. Stalin then asked whether Mandelstam was a master. Pasternak replied that as poets they were very different; that he admired Mandelstam's poetry but felt no affinity with it; but that in any case, this was not the point at all.

Here, in recounting the episode to me, Pasternak again embarked on one of his great metaphysical flights about the cosmic turning-points in the world's history; it was these that he wished to discuss with Stalin—it was of supreme importance that he should do so. I can easily imagine that he spoke in this vein to Stalin too. At any rate, Stalin asked him again whether he was or was not present when Mandelstam read the lampoon. Pasternak answered again that what mattered most was his indispensable meeting with Stalin, that it must happen soon, that everything depended on it, that they must speak about ultimate issues, about life and death. "If I were Mandelstam's friend, I should have known better how to defend him," said Stalin, and put down the receiver. Pasternak tried to ring back but, not surprisingly, failed to get through to the leader. The episode evidently preyed deeply upon him. He repeated to me the version I have just recounted on at least two other occasions, and told the story to other visitors, although, apparently, in different forms. His efforts to rescue Mandelstam, in particular his appeal to Bukharin, probably helped to preserve him at least for a time—Mandelstam was finally destroyed some years later—but Pasternak clearly felt, it may be without good reason, but as anyone not blinded by self-satisfaction or stupidity might feel, that perhaps another response might have done more for the condemned poet.[1]

He followed this story with accounts of other victims: Pil'nyak, who anxiously waited ("was constantly looking out the window") for an emissary to ask him to sign a denunciation of one of the men accused of treason in 1936, and because none came, realized that he, too, was doomed. He spoke of the circumstances of Tsvetaeva's suicide in 1941, which he thought might have been prevented if the literary bureaucrats had not behaved with such appalling heartlessness to her. He told the story of a man who asked him to sign an open letter condemning Marshal Tukhachevsky. When Pasternak refused and explained the reasons for his refusal, the man burst into tears, said that the poet was the noblest and most saintly human being whom he had ever met, embraced him fervently, and then went straight to the secret police, and denounced him.

Pasternak went on to say that despite the positive role which the Communist Party had played during the war, and not in Russia alone, he found the idea of any kind of relationship with it increasingly repellent: Russia was a gallery, a slave-ship, and the Party men were the overseers who whipped the rowers. Why, he wished to know, did a British Commonwealth diplomat then in Moscow, whom I surely knew, a man who knew some Russian and claimed to be a

---

1. Akhmatova and Nadezhda Mandelstam agreed to give him four out of five for his behavior in this case.

poet, and visited him occasionally, why did this person insist, on every possible and impossible occasion, that he, Pasternak, should get closer to the Party? He did not need gentlemen who came from the other side of the world to tell him what to do—could I tell the man that his visits were unwelcome? I promised that I would, but did not do so, partly for fear of rendering Pasternak's none too secure position still more precarious.

Pasternak reproached me, too; not, indeed, for seeking to impose my political or any other opinions on him—but for something that to him seemed almost as bad: here we both were, in Russia, and wherever one looked, everything was disgusting, appalling, an abominable pigsty, yet I seemed to be positively exhilarated by it: "You wander about," he said, "and look at everything with bemused eyes"—I was no better (he declared) than other foreign visitors who saw nothing, and suffered from absurd delusions, maddening to the poor miserable natives.

Pasternak was acutely sensitive to the charge of accommodating himself to the demands of the Party or the state—he seemed afraid that his mere survival might be attributed to some unworthy effort to placate the authorities, some squalid compromise of his integrity to escape persecution. He kept returning to this point, and went to absurd lengths to deny that he was capable of conduct of which no one who knew him could begin to conceive him to be guilty. One day he asked me whether I had heard anyone speak of his wartime volume of poems *On Early Trains* as a gesture of conformity with the prevailing orthodoxy. I said truthfully that I had not heard this, that it was an absurd suggestion.

Anna Akhmatova, who was bound to him by the deepest friendship and admiration, told me that, at the end of the war, when she was returning from Tashkent, to which she had been evacuated from Leningrad, she stopped in Moscow and visited Peredelkino. Within a few hours of arriving she received a message from Pasternak that he could not see her—he had a fever—he was in bed—it was impossible. On the next day the message was repeated. On the third day he appeared before her looking unusually well, with no trace of any ailment. The first thing he did was to ask her whether she had read this, the latest book of his poems. He put the question with so painful an expression on his face that she tactfully said that she had not, not yet; at which his face cleared, he looked vastly relieved, and they talked happily. He evidently felt ashamed, needlessly, of these poems. It seemed to him a kind of half-hearted effort to write civic poetry—there was nothing he disliked more intensely than this genre.

Yet, in 1945, he still had hopes of a great renewal of Russian life as a result of the cleansing storm that the war had seemed to him to be—a storm as transforming, in its own terrible fashion, as the Revolution itself, a vast cataclysm beyond our puny moral categories. Such vast mutations cannot, he held, be judged. One must think and think about them, and seek to understand as much of them as one can, all one's life; they are beyond good and evil, acceptance or rejection, doubt or assent; they must be accepted as elemental changes, earthquakes, tidal waves, transforming events, which are beyond all ethical and historical categories. So, too, the dark nightmare of betrayals, purges, massacres of the innocents, followed by an appalling war, seemed to him a necessary prelude to some inevitable, unheard-of victory of the spirit.

I did not see him again for eleven years. By 1956 his estrangement from his country's political establishment was complete. He could not speak of it, or its representatives, without a shudder. By that time his friend Olga Ivinskaya had been arrested, interrogated, maltreated, sent to a labor camp for five years. "Your Boris," the minister of state security, Abakumov, had said to her, "your Boris detests us, doesn't he?" "They were right," Pasternak said: "she could not and did not deny it." I had traveled to Peredelkino with Neuhaus and one of his sons by his first wife, who was now married to Pasternak. He repeated over and over again that Pasternak was a saint: that he was too unworldly—his hope that the Soviet authorities would permit the publication of *Doctor Zhivago* was plainly absurd—martyrdom of the author was far more likely. Pasternak was the greatest writer produced by Russia for decades, and he would be destroyed, as so many had been destroyed, by the state. This was an inheritance from the tsarist regime. Whatever the difference between the old and the new Russia, suspicion and persecution of writers and artists were common to both. His former wife Zinaida—now Pasternak's wife—had told him that Pasternak was determined to get his novel published somewhere. He had tried to dissuade him, but his words were in vain. If Pasternak mentioned the matter to me, would I—it was important—more than important—perhaps a matter of life and death, who could tell, even in these days?—would I try to persuade him to hold his hand? Neuhaus seemed to me to be right: Pasternak probably did need to be physically saved from himself.

By this time we had arrived at Pasternak's house. He was waiting for us by the gate and let Neuhaus go in, embraced me warmly and said that in the eleven years during which we had not met, much had happened, most of it very evil. He stopped and added, "Surely there is something you want to say to me?" I said, with monumental tactlessness (not to say unforgivable stupidity), "Boris Leonidovich, I am happy to see you looking so well. But the main thing is that you have survived. This seemed almost miraculous to some of us" (I was thinking of the anti-Jewish persecution of Stalin's last years). His face darkened and he looked at me with real anger: "I know what you are thinking," he said. "What am I thinking, Boris Leonidovich?" "I know, I know it, I know exactly what is in your mind," he replied in a breaking voice—it was very frightening—"do not prevaricate. I can see more clearly into your mind than I can into my own." "What am I thinking?" I asked again, more and more disturbed by his words. "You think—I know that you think—that I have done something for *them*." "I assure you, Boris Leonidovich," I replied, "that I never conceived of this—I have never heard this suggested by anyone, even as an idiotic joke." In the end he seemed to believe me. But he was visibly upset. Only after I had assured him that admiration for him, not only as a writer, but as a free and independent human being, was, among civilized people, world-wide, did he begin to return to his normal state. "At least," he said, "I can say, like Heine, 'I may not deserve to be remembered as a poet, but surely as a soldier in the battle for human freedom.'"

He took me to his study. There he thrust a thick envelope into my hands: "My book," he said, "it is all there. It is my last word. Please read it." I read *Doctor Zhivago* during the following night and day, and when two or three days later I saw him again, I asked what he intended to do with it. He told me that he had given it to an Italian communist, who worked in the Italian section of the Soviet radio, and at the same time was acting as an agent for the communist Italian publisher Feltrinelli. He had assigned world rights to Feltrinelli. He wished his novel, his testament, the most authentic, most complete of all his writings—his poetry was nothing in comparison (although the poems in the novel were, he thought, perhaps the best he had written)—he wished his work to travel over the entire world, to lay waste with fire (he quoted Pushkin's famous biblical line), to lay waste the hearts of men.

After the midday meal was over, his wife, Zinaida Nikolaevna, drew me aside and begged me with tears in her eyes to dissuade him from getting *Doctor Zhivago* published abroad. She did not wish her children to suffer; surely I knew what "they" were capable of? Moved by this plea, I spoke to the poet at the first opportunity. I promised to have microfilms of his novel made, to bury them in the four quarters of the globe, to bury copies in Oxford, in Valparaiso, in Tasmania, Cape Town, Haiti, Vancouver, Japan, so that copies might survive even if a nuclear war broke out—was he resolved to defy the Soviet authorities, had he considered the consequences?

For the second time during that week he showed a touch of real anger in talking to me. He told me that what I said was no doubt well intentioned, that he was touched by my concern for his own safety and that of his family (this was said a trifle ironically), but that he knew what he was doing; that I was worse than that importunate Commonwealth diplomat eleven years ago. He had spoken to his sons. They were prepared to suffer. I was not to mention the matter again. I had read the book, surely I realized what it, above all its dissemination, meant to him. I was shamed into silence.

After an interval, we talked about French literature, as often before. Since our last meeting he had procured Sartre's *La Nausée*, and found it unreadable, and its obscenity revolting. Surely after four centuries of creative genius this great nation could not have ceased to generate literature? Aragon was a time-server, Duhamel, Guéhenno were inconceivably tedious; was Malraux still writing? Before I could reply, one of his guests, a gentle, silent woman, a teacher who had recently returned after fifteen years in a labor camp, to which she had been condemned solely for teaching English, shyly asked whether Aldous Huxley had written anything since *Point Counter Point*. Was Virginia Woolf still writing?—she had never seen a book by her; but from an account in an old French newspaper which in some mysterious fashion had found its way into her camp, she thought that she might like her work.

It is difficult to convey the pleasure of being able to bring news of art and literature of the outer world to human beings so genuinely eager to receive it, so unlikely to obtain it from any other source. I told her and the assembled company all that I could of English, American, French writing. It was like speaking to the victims of ship-wreck on a desert island, cut off for decades from civilization. All they heard, they received as new, exciting, and delightful. The Georgian poet Titzian Tabidze, Pasternak's great friend, had perished in the Great Purge. His widow, Nina Tabidze, who was present, wanted to know whether Shakespeare, Ibsen, and Shaw were still great names in the Western theater. I told her that interest in Shaw had declined, but that Chekhov was greatly admired and often performed, and added that Akhmatova had said to me that she could not understand this worship of Chekhov. His world was uniformly drab. The sun never shone. No swords flashed. Everything was covered by a horrible gray mist. Chekhov's universe was a sea of mud with wretched human creatures caught in it helplessly. It was a travesty of life (I once heard Yeats express a similar sentiment: "Chekhov knows nothing of life and death," he said; "he does not know that the floor of heaven is full of the sound of the clashing of swords"). Pasternak said that Akhmatova was wholly mistaken. "Tell her when you see her—we cannot go to Leningrad freely, as you probably can—tell her from all of us here, that all Russian writers preach to the reader: even Turgenev tells him that time is a great healer and that kind of thing; Chekhov alone does not. He is a pure artist—everything is dissolved in art—he is our answer to Flaubert." He went on to say that Akhmatova would surely talk to me about Dostoevsky and attack Tolstoy. But Tolstoy was right about Dostoevsky, that his novels were a dreadful mess, a mixture of chauvinism and hysterical religion: "Tell Anna Andreevna that, and from me!" But when I saw Akhmatova again, in Oxford in 1965, I thought it best not to report his judgment: she might have wished to answer him. But Pasternak was in his grave. In fact, she did speak to me of Dostoevsky with the most passionate admiration.

III

And this brings me to my meeting with the poet Anna Akhmatova. I had been introduced to her poems by Maurice Bowra, and longed to meet her. In November 1945 I went from Moscow to Leningrad. I had not seen the city since 1919, when I was ten years old and my family was allowed to return to our native city of Riga, the capital of a then independent republic. In Leningrad my recollections of childhood became fabulously vivid. I was inexpressibly moved by the look of the streets, the houses, the statues, the embankments, the market places, the suddenly familiar, still broken, railings of a little shop, in which samovars were mended, below the house in which we had lived. The inner yard of the house looked as sordid and abandoned as it had done during the first years of the Revolution. My memories of specific events, episodes, experiences, came between me and the physical reality. It was as if I had walked into a legendary city, myself at once part of the vivid, half-remembered legend, and yet, at the same time, viewing it from some outside vantage point. The city had been greatly damaged, but still in 1945 remained indescribably beautiful (it seemed wholly restored by the time I saw it again, eleven years later). I made my way to the Writers' Bookshop in the Nevsky Prospekt. While looking at the books, I fell into casual conversation with a man who was turning over the leaves of a book of poems. He turned out to be a well-known critic and literary historian. We talked about recent events. He described the terrible ordeal of the siege of Leningrad and the martyrdom and heroism of many of its inhabitants, and said that some had died of cold and hunger, others, mostly the younger ones, had survived. Some had been evacuated. I asked him about the fate of writers in Leningrad. He said, "You mean Zoshchenko and Akhmatova?" Akhmatova to me was a figure from a remote past. Maurice Bowra, who had translated some of her poems, spoke about her to me as someone not heard of since the First World War. "Is Akhmatova still alive?" I asked. "Akhmatova, Anna Andreevna?" he said: "Why yes, of course. She lives not far from here on the Fontanka, in Fontanny Dom [Fountain House]; would you like to meet her?" It was as if I had suddenly been invited to meet Miss Christina Rossetti. I could hardly speak. I mumbled that I should indeed like to meet her. "I shall telephone her," my new acquaintance said. He returned to tell me that she would receive us at three that afternoon. I was to return to the bookshop, and we would go together.

I returned at the appointed hour. The critic and I left the bookshop, turned left, crossed the Anichkov Bridge, and turned left again, along the embankment of the Fontanka. Fountain House, the palace of the Sheremetevs, is a magnificent late baroque building, with gates of exquisite ironwork for which Leningrad is famous, and built around a spacious court—not unlike the quadrangle of a large Oxford or Cambridge college. We climbed up one of the steep, dark staircases, to an upper floor, and were admitted to Akhmatova's room. It was very barely furnished—virtually everything in it had, I gathered, been taken away—looted or sold—during the siege. There was a small table, three or four chairs, a wooden chest, a sofa, and, above the unlit stove, a drawing by Modigliani. A stately, gray-haired lady, a white shawl draped about her shoulders, slowly rose to greet us.

Anna Andreevna Akhmatova was immensely dignified, with unhurried gestures, a noble head, beautiful, somewhat severe features, and an expression of immense sadness. I bowed. It seemed appropriate, for she looked and moved like a tragic queen. I thanked her for receiving me, and said that people in the West would be glad to know that she was in good health, for nothing had been heard of her for many years. "Oh, but an article on me has appeared in the *Dublin Review*," she said, "and a thesis is being written about my work, I am told, in Bologna." She had a friend with her, an academic lady of some sort, and there was polite conversation for some minutes. Then Akhmatova asked me about the ordeal of London during the bombing: I answered as best I could, feeling acutely shy and constricted by her distant, somewhat regal manner. Suddenly I heard what sounded like my first name being shouted somewhere outside. I ignored this for a while—it could only be an illusion—but the shouting became louder and the word "Isaiah" could be clearly heard. I went to the window and looked out, and saw a man whom I recognized as Randolph Churchill. He was standing in the middle of the great court, looking like a tipsy undergraduate, and screaming my name. I stood rooted to the floor for some seconds. Then I collected myself, muttered an apology, and ran down the stairs. My only thought was to prevent Churchill from coming to the room. My companion, the critic, ran after me anxiously. When we emerged into the court, Churchill came towards me and greeted me effusively: "Mr. X," I said mechanically, "I do not suppose that you have met Mr. Randolph Churchill?" The critic froze, his expression changed from bewilderment to horror, and he left as rapidly as he could. I have no notion whether I was followed by agents of the secret police, but there could be no doubt that Randolph Churchill was. It was this untoward event that caused absurd rumors to circulate in Leningrad that a foreign delegation had arrived to persuade Akhmatova to leave Russia; that Winston Churchill, a lifelong admirer of the poet, was sending a special aircraft to take Akhmatova to England, and so on.

Randolph, whom I had not met since we were undergraduates at Oxford, subsequently explained that he was in Moscow as a journalist on behalf of the North American Newspaper Alliance. He had come to Leningrad as part of his assignment. On arriving at the Hotel Astoria, his first concern had been to get the pot of caviar which he had acquired into an icebox: but, as he knew no Russian, and his interpreter had disappeared, his cries for help had finally brought down a representative of the British Council. She saw to his caviar and, in the course of general conversation, told him that I was in the city. He said that I might make an excellent substitute interpreter, and unfortunately discovered from the British Council lady where I was to be found. The rest followed. When he reached Fountain House, he adopted a method which had served him well during his days in Christ Church,[2] and, I dare say, on other occasions; "and," he said with a winning smile, "it worked." I detached myself from him as quickly as I could, and after obtaining her number from the book-seller, telephoned Akhmatova to offer an explanation of my precipi-tate departure, and to apologize for it. I asked if I might be allowed to call on her again. "I shall wait for you at nine this evening," she answered.

When I returned, a learned lady, an Assyriologist, was also pres-ent who asked me a great many questions about English universities and their organization. Akhmatova was plainly uninterested and, for the most part, silent. Shortly before midnight the Assyriologist left, and then Akhmatova began to ask me about old friends who had emigrated—some of whom I might know. (She was sure of that, she told me later. In personal relationships, she assured me, her intu-ition—almost second sight—never failed her.) I did indeed know some of them. We talked about the composer Artur Lurié, whom I had met in America during the war. He had been an intimate friend of hers, and had set to music some of her, and of Mandelstam's, po-etry. She asked about Boris Anrep, the mosaicist (whom I had never met): I knew little about him, only that he had decorated the floor of the entrance hall of the National Gallery with the figures of cele-brated persons—Bertrand Russell, Virginia Woolf, Greta Garbo,

---

2. His Oxford college.

Clive Bell, Lydia Lopokhova, and the like. Twenty years later I was able to tell her that an image of herself had been added to them by Anrep. She showed me a ring with a black stone which Anrep had given her in 1917.

She had, she said, met only one foreigner—a Pole—since the First World War. She asked after various other friends—Salomé Andronikova, to whom Mandelstam dedicated one of his most famous poems; Stravinsky's wife, Vera; the poets Vyacheslav Ivanov and Georgi Adamovich. I answered as best I could. She spoke of her visits to Paris before the First World War, of her friendship with Amedeo Modigliani, whose drawing of her hung over the fireplace—one of many (the rest had perished during the siege). She described her childhood on the shores of the Black Sea, a pagan, unbaptized land, she called it, where one felt close to an ancient, half-Greek, half-barbarian, deeply un-Russian, culture. She spoke of her first husband, the celebrated poet Gumilev. She was convinced that he had not taken part in the monarchist conspiracy for which he had been executed; Gorky, who had been asked by many writers to intervene on his behalf, apparently did nothing to save him. She had not seen him for some time before his condemnation—they had been divorced some years before. Her eyes had tears in them when she described the harrowing circumstances of his death.

After a silence, she asked me whether I would like to hear her poetry. But before doing this, she said that she wished to recite two cantos from Byron's *Don Juan* to me, for they were relevant to what would follow. Even if I had known the poem well, I could not have told which cantos she had chosen, for although she read English fairly freely, her pronunciation of it made it impossible to understand more than a word or two. She closed her eyes and spoke the lines from memory, with intense emotion. I rose and looked out of the window to conceal my embarrassment. Perhaps, I thought afterwards, that is how we now read classical Greek and Latin. Yet we, too, are moved by the words, which, as we pronounce them, might have been wholly unintelligible to their authors and audiences. Then she read from her book of poems—*Anno Domini, The White Flock, Out of Six Books*—"Poems like these, but far better than mine," she said, "were the cause of the death of the best poet of our time, whom I loved and who loved me..."—whether she meant Gumilev or Mandelstam I could not tell, for she broke down in tears, and could not go on reading.

There are recordings of her readings, and I shall not attempt to describe them. She read the (at that time) still unfinished *Poem Without a Hero*. I realized even then that I was listening to a work of genius. I do not suppose that I understood that many-faceted and most magical poem and its deeply personal allusions any better than when I read it now. She made no secret of the fact that it was intended as a kind of final memorial to her life as a poet, to the past of the city—St. Petersburg—which was part of her being, and, in the form of a Twelfth Night carnival procession of masked figures en travesti, to her friends, and to their lives and destinies and her own—a kind of artistic *nunc dimittis* before the inescapable end which would not be long in coming. It is a mysterious and deeply evocative work: a tumulus of learned commentary is inexorably rising over it. Soon it may be buried under its weight.

Then she read the *Requiem*, from a manuscript. She broke off and spoke of the years 1937-1938, when both her husband and her son had been arrested and sent to prison camps (this was to happen again), of the queues of women who waited day and night, week after week, month after month, for news of their husbands, brothers, fathers, sons, for permission to send food or letters to them. No news ever came. No messages ever reached them. A pall of death in life hung over the cities of the Soviet Union, while the torture and slaughter of millions of innocents were going on. She spoke in a dry, matter-of-fact voice, occasionally interrupting herself with "No, I cannot, it is no good, you come from a society of human beings, whereas here we are divided into human beings and...." Then a long silence: "And even now...." She would once more be silent. I asked about Mandelstam: she paused, her eyes filled with tears, and she begged me not to speak of him: "After he slapped Aleksey Tolstoy's face, it was all over...." It took some time for her to collect herself. Then in a totally changed voice, she said, "Aleksey Tolstoy wore lilac shirts *à la russe* when we were in Tashkent. He spoke of the marvelous time he and I would have together when we came back. He was a very gifted and interesting writer, a scoundrel, full of charm, and a man of stormy temperament. He is dead now. He was capable of anything, anything. He was a wild adventurer. He only liked youth, power, vitality. He didn't finish his *Peter the First* because he said that he could only deal with Peter as a young man; what was he to do with all those people when they grew old? He was a kind of Dolokhov. He called me Annushka. That made me wince, but I liked him very much, even though he was the cause of the death of the best poet of our time, whom I loved, and who loved me." (Her words were identical with those she had used earlier; it now seemed clear to me to whom, on both occasions, she was referring.)

It was, I think, by now about three in the morning. She showed no sign of wishing me to leave, and I was far too moved and absorbed to stir. She left the room and came back with a dish of boiled potatoes. It was all she had, and she was embarrassed at the poverty of her hospitality. I begged her to let me write down the *Poem Without a Hero* and *Requiem*: she said there was no need for that. A volume of her collected verse was due to appear the next February. It was all in proof. She would send me a copy. The Party, as we know, ruled otherwise. She was denounced by Zhdanov (in a phrase which he had not invented) as "half nun, half harlot." This put her beyond the official pale.

We talked about Russian literature. After dismissing Chekhov because of the absence in his world of heroism and martyrdom, of depth and darkness and sublimity, we talked about *Anna Karenina*. "Why did Tolstoy make her commit suicide? As soon as she leaves Karenin, everything changes. She suddenly turns into a fallen woman, a *traviata*, a prostitute. Who punishes Anna? God? No, not God—society—that same society whose hypocrisies Tolstoy is constantly denouncing. In the end he tells us that Anna repels even Vronsky. Tolstoy is lying. He knew better than that. The morality of *Anna Karenina* is the morality of Tolstoy's Moscow aunts, of philistine conventions. It is all connected with his personal vicissitudes. When Tolstoy was happily married he wrote *War and Peace* which celebrates the family. After he started hating Sophia Andreevna, but could not divorce her, because divorce is condemned by society, and maybe by the peasants too, he wrote *Anna Karenina*, and punished Anna for leaving her husband. When he was old, and felt guilt for still lusting violently after peasant girls, he wrote *The Kreutzer Sonata* and forbade sex altogether."

These were her words. I do not know how seriously they were meant, but Akhmatova's dislike of Tolstoy's sermons was genuine— she regarded him as a monster of vanity, and an enemy of freedom. She worshipped Dostoevsky and, like him, despised Turgenev. And, after Dostoevsky, Kafka, whom she read in English translations. ("He wrote for me and about me," she told me years afterward in Oxford—"Kafka is a greater writer than even Joyce and Eliot. He did not understand everything; only Pushkin did that.") She then spoke to me about Pushkin's *Egyptian Nights*, and about the pale stranger in that story who improvised verse on themes supplied by the audience. The virtuoso, in her opinion, was the Polish poet Adam Mickewiecz. Pushkin's relation to him became ambivalent. The Polish issue divided them. But Pushkin always recognized genius in his contemporaries. Blok was like that—with his mad eyes and marvelous genius, he too could have been an *improvisateur*. She said that Blok had never liked her, but that every schoolmistress in Russia believed, and would doubtless go on believing, that they had had a love affair. Historians of literature believed this too. All this, in her opinion, was based on her poem *A Visit to the Poet*, dedicated to Blok; and, perhaps, also on the poem on the death of *The Grey-Eyed King*, although that was written more than ten years before Blok died. Blok liked none of the Acmeists, of whom she was one. He did not like Pasternak either.

She then spoke about Pasternak, whom she loved deeply, though she had never been in love with him. After Mandelstam's and Tsvetaeva's deaths, they were alone. The knowledge that the other was alive and at work was a source of infinite comfort to both of them. They criticized each other freely, but allowed no one else to do so. The passionate devotion of countless men and women in the Soviet Union who knew their verse by heart, and copied it and circulated it, was a source of pride to them. But they both remained in exile. The thought of emigration was hateful to both. They longed to visit the West, but not if it meant that they would be unable to return. Their deep patriotism was not tinged by nationalism. Akhmatova was not prepared to move. No matter what horrors might be in store, she would never abandon Russia.

She spoke of her childhood, her marriages, her relationships with others, of the rich artistic life in Petersburg before the First World War. She had no doubt that the culture of the West, especially now, in 1945, was far superior to it. She spoke about the great poet Annensky, who had taught her more even than Gumilev, and died largely ignored by editors and critics, a great forgotten master. She spoke about her loneliness and isolation. Leningrad, after the war, was for her nothing but the graveyard of her friends—it was like the aftermath of a forest fire, the few charred trees made the desolation still more desolate. She lived by translating. She had begged to be allowed to translate the letters of Rubens, not those of Romain Rolland. After unheard-of obstacles, permission was finally granted. I asked her what the Renaissance meant to her—was it a real historical past, or an idealized vision, an imaginary world? She replied that it was the latter. She felt nostalgia for it—that longing for a universal culture of which Mandelstam had spoken, as Goethe and Schlegel had thought of it—a longing for what had been transmuted into art and thought— nature, love, death, despair, and martyrdom—a reality which had no history, nothing outside itself. She spoke in a calm, even voice, like a remote princess in exile, proud, unhappy, unapproachable, often in words of the most moving eloquence.

The account of the unrelieved tragedy of her life went beyond anything which anyone had ever described to me in spoken words; the recollection of them is still vivid and painful to me. I asked her whether she intended to compose a record of her literary life. She replied that her poetry was that, in particular the *Poem Without a Hero*, which she read to me again. Once more I begged her to let me write it down. Once again she declined. Our conversation, which touched on intimate details of both her life and my own, wandered from literature and art, and lasted until late in the morning of the following day. I saw her again when I was leaving the Soviet Union to go home by way of Leningrad and Helsinki. I went to say goodbye to her on the afternoon of January 5, 1946, and she then gave me one of her collections of verse, with a new poem inscribed on the flyleaf— the poem that was later to form the second in the cycle entitled *Cinque*. I realized that this poem, in this, its first version, had been directly inspired by our earlier meeting. There are other references and allusions to our meetings, in *Cinque* and elsewhere.

I did not see her on my next visit to the Soviet Union in 1956. Her son, who had been re-arrested, had been released from his prison camp earlier that year, and Pasternak told me that she felt acutely nervous about seeing foreigners except by official order, but that she wished me to telephone her; this was far safer, for all her telephone conversations were monitored. Over the telephone she told me something of her experiences as a condemned writer; of the turning away by some whom she had considered faithful friends, of the nobility and courage of others. She had re-read Chekov, and said that at least in *Ward No. 6* he had accurately described her situation, and that of many others. Meanwhile her translations from the classical Korean verse had been published—"You can imagine how much Korean I know; it is a selection; not selected by me. There is no need for you to read it."

When we met in Oxford in 1965 Akhmatova told me that Stalin had been personally enraged by the fact that she had allowed me to visit her: "So our nun now receives visits from foreign spies," he is alleged to have remarked, and followed this with obscenities which she could not at first bring herself to repeat to me. The fact that I had never worked in any intelligence organization was irrelevant. All members of foreign missions were spies to Stalin. Of course, she said, the old man was by then out of his mind, in the grip of pathological paranoia. In Oxford she told me that she was convinced that Stalin's fury, which we had caused, had unleashed the cold war—that she and I had changed the history of mankind. She meant this quite literally and insisted on its truth. She saw herself and me as world-historical personages chosen by destiny to play our fateful part in a cosmic conflict, and this is reflected in her poems of this time. It was intrinsic to her entire historico-philosophical vision, from which much of her poetry flowed.

She told me that after her journey to Italy in the previous year, when she had been awarded a literary prize, she was visited by officials of the Soviet secret police, who asked her for her impressions of Rome. She replied that Rome seemed to her to be a city where paganism was still at war with Christianity. "What war?" she was asked. "Was the USA mentioned? Are Russian émigrés involved?" What should she answer when similar questions were put to her about England and Oxford? For to Russia she would return no matter what awaited her there. The Soviet regime was the established order of her country. With it she had lived, and with it she would die. That is what being a Russian meant.

We returned to Russian poetry. She spoke contemptuously of well-known young poets, favored by the Soviet authorities. One of the most famous of these, who was in England at the time, had sent her a telegram to Oxford to congratulate her on her honorary doctorate. I was there when it arrived. She read it, and angrily threw it in the waste-paper basket—"They are all little bandits, prostitutes of their gifts, and exploiters of public taste. Mayakovsky's influence has been fatal to them all. Mayakovsky shouted at the top of his voice because it was natural to him to do so. He could not help it. His imitators have adopted his manner as a genre. They are vulgar declaimers with not a spark of true poetry in them."

There were many gifted poets in Russia now: the best among them was Joseph Brodsky, whom she had, she said, brought up by hand, and whose poetry had in part been published: a noble poet in deep disfavor, with all that that implied. There were others, too, marvelously gifted—but their names would mean nothing to me—poets whose verses could not be published, and whose very existence was testimony to the unexhausted life of the imagination in Russia: "They will eclipse us all," she said, "believe me, Pasternak and I and Mandelstam and Tsvetaeva, all of us are the end of a long period of elaboration which began in the nineteenth century. My friends and I thought we spoke with the voice of the twentieth century. But these new poets constitute a new beginning—behind bars now, but they will escape and astonish the world." She spoke at some length in this prophetic vein, and returned again to Mayakovsky, driven to despair, betrayed by his friends, but, for a while, the true voice, the trumpet, of his people, though a fatal example to others; she herself owed nothing to him, but much to Annensky, the purest and finest of poets, remote from the hurly-burly of literary politics, largely neglected by avant-garde journals, fortunate to have died when he did. He was not read widely in his lifetime, but then this was the fate of other great poets—the present generation was far more sensitive to poetry than her own had been: who cared, who truly cared about Blok or Bely or Vyacheslav Ivanov in 1910? Or, for that matter, about herself and the poets of her group? But today the young knew it all by heart—she was still getting letters from young people, many of them from silly, ecstatic girls, but the sheer number of them was surely evidence of something.

Pasternak received even more of these, and liked them better. Had I met his friend Olga Ivinskaya? I had not. She found both Pasternak's wife, Zinaida, and his mistress equally unbearable, but Boris Leonidovich himself was a magical poet, one of the great poets of the Russian land: every sentence he wrote, in verse and prose, spoke with his authentic voice, unlike any other she had ever heard. Blok and Pasternak were divine poets; no modern Frenchman, no Englishman, not Valéry, not Eliot, could compare with them—Baudelaire, Shelley, Leopardi, that was the company to which they belonged. Like all great poets, they had little sense of the quality of others—Pasternak often praised inferior critics, discovered imaginary hidden gifts, encouraged all kinds of minor figures—decent writers but without talent—he had a mythological sense of history, in which quite worthless people sometimes played mysterious, significant roles—like Evgraf in

Doctor Zhivago (she vehemently denied that this mysterious figure was in any respect based on Stalin; she evidently found this impossible to contemplate). He did not really read contemporary authors he was prepared to praise—not Bagritsky or Aseev, not even Mandelstam (whom he could not bear, though of course he did what he could for him when he was in trouble), nor her own work—he wrote her wonderful letters about her poetry, but the letters were about himself, not her—she knew that they were sublime fantasies which had little to do with her: "Perhaps all great poets are like this."

Pasternak's compliments naturally made those who received them very happy, but this was delusive; he was a generous giver, but not truly interested in the work of others: interested, of course, in Shakespeare, Goethe, the French Symbolists, Rilke, perhaps Proust, but "not in any of us." She said that she missed Pasternak's existence every day of her life; they had never been in love, but they loved one another deeply and this irritated his wife. She then spoke of the "blank" years during which she was officially out of account in the Soviet Union—between the mid-Twenties until the late Thirties. She said that when she was not translating, she read Russian poets: Pushkin constantly, of course, but also Odoevsky, Lermontov, Baratynsky—she thought Baratynsky's *Autumn* was a work of pure genius; and she had recently reread Velemir Khelbnikov—mad but marvelous.

I asked her if she would ever annotate the *Poem Without a Hero*: the allusions might be unintelligible to those who did not know the life it was concerned with; did she wish them to remain in darkness? She answered that when those who knew the world about which she spoke were overtaken by senility or death, the poem would die too; it would be buried with her and her century; it was not written for eternity, nor even for posterity: the past alone had significance for poets—childhood most of all—those were the emotions that they wished to re-create and re-live. Vaticination, odes to the future, even

Pushkin's great epistle to Chaadaev, were a form of declamatory rhetoric, a striking of grandiose attitudes, the poet's eye peering into a dimly discernible future, a pose which she despised.

She knew, she said, that she had not long to live. Doctors had made it plain to her that her heart was weak. Above all, she did not wish to be pitied. She had faced horrors, and had known the most terrible depths of grief. She had exacted from her friends the promise that they would not allow the faintest gleam of pity for her to occur; hatred, insult, contempt, misunderstanding, persecution, she could bear, but not sympathy if it was mingled with compassion. Her pride and dignity were very great.

The detachment and impersonality with which she seemed to speak only partially disguised her passionate convictions and moral judgments, against which there was plainly no appeal. Her accounts of personalities and lives were compounded of sharp insight into the moral center of characters and situations (she did not spare her friends in this respect) together with fixed ideas, from which she could not be moved. She knew that our meeting had had serious historical consequences. She knew that the poet Georgi Ivanov, whom she accused of having written lying memoirs after he emigrated, had at one time been a police spy in the pay of the tsarist government. She knew that the poet Nekrasov in the nineteenth century had also been a government agent; that the poet Annensky had been hounded to death by his literary enemies. These beliefs had no apparent foundation in fact—they were intuitive, but they were not senseless, not sheer fantasies; they were elements in a coherent conception of her own and her nation's life and fate, of the central issues which Pasternak had wanted to discuss with Stalin, the vision which sustained and shaped her imagination and her art. She was not a visionary; she had, for the most part, a strong sense of reality. She described the literary and social scene in Petersburg before the First World War, and her part in it, with a sober realism and sharpness of detail which made it totally credible.

Akhmatova lived in terrible times, during which, according to Nadezhda Mandelstam, she behaved with heroism. She did not in public, nor indeed to me in private, utter a single word against the Soviet regime. But her entire life was what Herzen once described Russian literature as being—one continuous indictment of Russian reality.

The worship of her memory in the Soviet Union today, undeclared but widespread, has, so far as I know, no parallel. Her unyielding passive resistance to what she regarded as unworthy of her country and herself transformed her into a figure (as Belinsky once predicted about Herzen) not merely in Russian literature, but in the Russian history of our time.

My meetings and conversations with Boris Pasternak and Anna Akhmatova; my realization of the conditions, scarcely describable, under which they lived and worked, and of the treatment to which they were subjected; and the fact that I was allowed to enter into a personal relationship, indeed, friendship, with them both, affected me profoundly and permanently changed my outlook. When I see their names in print, or hear them mentioned, I remember vividly the expressions on their faces, their gestures and their words. When I read their writings I can, to this day, hear the sound of their voices.

—November 20, 1980

IO

JOSEPH BRODSKY
ON NADEZHDA MANDELSTAM

OF THE EIGHTY-ONE years of her life, Nadezhda Mandelstam spent nineteen as the wife of Russia's greatest poet in this century, Osip Mandelstam, and forty-two as his widow. The rest was childhood and youth. In educated circles, especially among the literati, being the widow of a great man is enough to provide an identity. This is especially so in Russia, where in the Thirties and in the Forties the regime was producing writers' widows with such efficiency that in the middle of the Sixties there were enough of them around to organize a trade union.

"Nadya is the luckiest widow," Anna Akhmatova used to say, having in mind the universal recognition coming to Osip Mandelstam at about that time. The focus of this remark was, understandably, on her fellow poet, and right though she was this was the view from the outside. By the time this recognition began to arrive, Mrs. Mandelstam was already in her sixties, her health extremely precarious and her means meager. Besides, for all the universality of that recognition, it did not include the fabled "one-sixth of the entire planet," i.e., Russia itself. Behind her were already two decades of widowhood, utter deprivation, the Great (obliterating any personal loss) War, and the daily fear of being grabbed by the agents of state security as a wife of an enemy of the people. Short of death, anything that followed could only mean respite.

I met her for the first time precisely then, in the winter of 1962, in the city of Pskov, where together with a couple of friends I went to take a look at the local churches (the finest, in my view, in the empire). Having learned about our intentions to travel to that city, Anna Akhmatova suggested we visit Nadezhda Mandelstam, who was teaching English at the local pedagogical institute, and gave us several books for her. That was the first time I heard her name: I didn't know that she existed.

She was living in a small communal apartment consisting of two rooms. The first room was occupied by a woman whose name, ironically enough, was Nietsvetaeva (literally: Non-Tsvetaeva), the second was Mrs. Mandelstam's. It was eight square meters large, the size of an average American bathroom. Most of the space was taken up by a cast-iron twin-sized bed; there were also two wicker chairs, a wardrobe chest with a small mirror, and an all-purpose bedside table, on which sat plates with the leftovers of her supper and, next to the plates, an open paperback copy of *The Hedgehog and the Fox*, by Isaiah Berlin. The presence of this red-covered book in this tiny cell, and the fact that she didn't hide it under the pillow at the sound of the doorbell, meant precisely this: the beginning of respite.

The book, as it turned out, was sent to her by Akhmatova, who for nearly half the century remained the closest friend of the Mandelstams: first of both of them, later of Nadezhda alone. Twice a widow herself (her first husband, the poet Nikolai Gumilev, was shot in 1921 by the Cheka—the maiden name of the KGB; the second, the art historian Nikolai Punin, died in a concentration camp belonging to the same establishment), Akhmatova helped Nadezhda Mandelstam in every way possible, and during the war years literally saved her life by smuggling Nadezhda into Tashkent, where some of the writers had been evacuated, and by sharing with her the daily rations. Even with her two husbands killed by the regime, with her son languishing in the camps (for about sixteen years, if I am not mistaken), Akhmatova was somewhat better off than Nadezhda Mandelstam, if only because she was recognized, however reluctantly, as a writer, and was allowed to live in Leningrad and Moscow. For the wife of an enemy of the people big cities were simply off limits.

For decades this woman was on the run, darting through the backwaters and provincial towns of the big empire, settling down in a new place only to take off at the first sign of danger. The status of nonperson gradually became her second nature. She was a small woman, of slim build, and with the passage of years she shriveled more and more, as though trying to turn herself into something weightless, something easily pocketed in the moment of flight. Similarly, she had virtually no possessions; no furniture, no art objects, no library. The books, even foreign books, never stayed in her hands for long: after being read or glanced through they would be passed on to someone else—the way it ought to be with books. In the years of her utmost affluence, at the end of the Sixties and the beginning of the Seventies, the most expensive item in her one-room apartment in the outskirts of Moscow was a cuckoo clock on the kitchen wall. A thief would be disillusioned here; so would be those with an order for search.

In those "affluent" years following the publication in the West of her two volumes of memoirs[1] that kitchen became the place of veritable pilgrimages. Nearly every other night the best of what survived or came to life in the post-Stalin era in Russia gathered around the long wooden table which was ten times bigger than the bedstead in

---

1. Translated as *Hope Against Hope* and *Hope Abandoned* (both published by Atheneum, in 1970 and 1973, and translated by Max Hayward).

Pskov. It almost seemed that she was about to make up for decades of being a pariah. I doubt, though, that she did, and somehow I remember her better in that small room in Pskov, or sitting on the edge of a couch in Akhmatova's apartment in Leningrad, where she would come from time to time illegally from Pskov, or emerging from the depth of the corridor in Shklovsky's apartment in Moscow, where she perched before she got the place of her own. Perhaps I remember that more clearly because there she was more in her element as an outcast, a fugitive, "the beggar-friend," as Osip Mandelstam calls her in one of his poems, and that is what she remained for the rest of her life.

There is something quite breathtaking in the realization that she wrote those two volumes of hers at the age of sixty-five. In the Mandelstam family Osip was the writer, she wasn't. If she wrote anything before those volumes, it was letters to her friends or appeals to the Supreme Court. Nor is hers the case of someone reviewing a long and eventful life in the tranquillity of retirement. Because her sixty-five years were not exactly normal. It's not for nothing that in the Soviet penal system there is a paragraph specifying that in certain camps a year of serving counts for three. By this token, the lives of many Russians in this century came to approximate in length those of Biblical patriarchs. With whom she had one more thing in common: devotion to justice.

Yet it wasn't this devotion to justice alone that made her sit down at the age of sixty-five and use her time of respite for writing these books. What brought them into existence was a recapitulation, on the scale of one, of the same process that once before had taken place in the history of Russian literature. I have in mind the emergence of great Russian prose in the second half of the nineteenth century. That prose, which appears as though out of nowhere, as an effect without traceable cause, was in fact simply a spin-off of the nineteenth century's Russian poetry. It set the tone for all subsequent writing in Russian, and the best work of Russian fiction can be regarded as a distant echo and meticulous elaboration of the psychological and lexical subtlety displayed by the Russian poetry of the first quarter of that century. "Most of Dostoevsky's characters," Anna Akhmatova used to say, "are aged Pushkin heroes, Onegins and so forth."

Poetry always precedes prose, and so it did in the life of Nadezhda Mandelstam, and in more ways than one. As a writer, as well as a person, she is a creation of two poets with whom her life was linked inexorably: Osip Mandelstam and Anna Akhmatova. And not only because the first was her husband and the second her lifelong friend. After all, forty years of widowhood could dim the happiest memories (and in the case of this marriage they were few and far between, if only because this marriage coincided with the economic devastation of the country, caused by revolution, civil war, and the first five-year plans). Similarly, there were years when she wouldn't see Akhmatova at all, and a letter would be the last thing to confide to. Paper, in general, was dangerous. What strengthened the bond of that marriage as well as of that friendship was a technicality: the necessity to commit to memory what could not be committed to paper, i.e., the poems of both authors.

In doing so in that "pre-Gutenberg epoch," in Akhmatova's words, Nadezhda Mandelstam certainly wasn't alone. However, repeating day and night the words of her dead husband was undoubtedly connected not only with comprehending them more and more but also with resurrecting his very voice, the intonations peculiar only to him, with a however fleeting sensation of his presence, with the realization that he kept his part of that "for better or for worse" deal, especially its second half. The same went for the poems of the physically often absent Akhmatova, for once set in motion this mechanism of memorization won't come to a halt. The same went for other authors, for certain ideas, for ethical principles—for everything that couldn't survive otherwise.

And gradually those things grew on her. If there is any substitute for love, it's memory. To memorize, then, is to restore intimacy. Gradually the lines of those poets became her mentality, became her identity. They supplied her not only with the plane of regard or angle of vision; more important, they became her linguistic norm. So when she set out to write her books, she was bound to gauge—by that time already unwittingly, instinctively—her sentences against theirs. The clarity and remorselessness of her pages, while reflecting the character of her mind, are also inevitable stylistic consequences of the poetry that had shaped that mind. Both in their content and style, her books are but a postscript to the supreme version of language which poetry essentially is and which became her flesh through learning her husband's lines by heart.

To borrow W. H. Auden's phrase, great poetry "hurt" her into prose. It really did, because those two poets' heritage could be developed or elaborated upon only by prose. In poetry they could be followed only by epigones. Which has happened. In other words, Nadezhda Mandelstam's prose was the only available medium for the language itself to avoid stagnation. Similarly, it was the only medium available for the psyche formed by that poets' use of language. Her books, thus, were not so much memoirs and guides to the lives of two great poets, however superbly they performed these functions; these books elucidated the consciousness of the nation. Of the part of it, at least, that could get a copy.

Small wonder, then, that this elucidation results in an indictment of the system. These two volumes by Mrs. Mandelstam indeed amount to a Day of Judgment on earth for her age and for its literature—a judgment administered all the more rightfully since it was this age that had undertaken the construction of earthly paradise. A lesser wonder, too, that these memoirs, the second volume especially, were not liked on either side of the Kremlin Wall. The authorities, I must say, were more honest in their reaction than the intelligentsia: they simply made possession of these books an offense punishable by law. As for the intelligentsia, especially in Moscow, it went into actual turmoil over Nadezhda Mandelstam's charges against many of its illustrious and not so illustrious members of virtual complicity with the regime, and the human flood in her kitchen significantly ebbed.

There were open and semi-open letters, indignant resolutions not to shake hands, friendships and marriages collapsing over whether she was right or wrong to consider this or that person an informer. A prominent dissident declared, shaking his beard: "She shat over our entire generation"; others would rush to their dachas and lock themselves up there, to tap out anti-memoirs. This was already the beginning of the Seventies, and some six years later these same people would become equally split over Solzhenitsyn's attitudes toward the Jews.

There is something in the consciousness of literati that cannot stand the notion of someone's moral authority. They resign themselves to the existence of a First Party Secretary, or of a Führer, as to a necessary evil, but they would eagerly question a prophet. This is so, presumably, because being told that you are a slave is less disheartening news than being told that morally you are a zero. After all, a fallen dog shouldn't be kicked. However, a prophet kicks the fallen dog not to finish it off but to get it back on its feet. The resistance to those kicks, the questioning of a writer's assertions and charges, comes not from the desire for truth but from the intellectual smugness of slavery. All the worse, then, for the literati when the authority is not only moral but also cultural—as it was in Nadezhda Mandelstam's case.

I'd like to venture here one step further. By itself reality per se isn't worth a damn. It's perception that promotes reality to meaning. And there is a hierarchy among perceptions (and, correspondingly, among meanings), with the ones acquired through the most refined and sensitive prisms sitting at the top. Refinement and sensitivity are imparted to such a prism by the only source of their supply: by culture, by civilization, whose main tool is language. The evaluation of reality made through such a prism—the acquisition of which is one goal of the species—is therefore the most accurate, perhaps even the most just. (Cries of "Unfair!" and "Elitist!" that may follow the aforesaid from, of all places, the local campuses must be left unheeded, for culture is "elitist" by definition, and the application of democratic principles in the sphere of knowledge leads to equating wisdom with idiocy.)

It's the possession of this prism supplied to her by the best Russian poetry of the twentieth century, and not the uniqueness of the size of her grief, that makes Nadezhda Mandelstam's statement about her piece of reality unchallengeable. It's an abominable fallacy that suffering makes for greater art. Suffering blinds, deafens, ruins, and often kills. Osip Mandelstam was a great poet *before* the revolution. So was Anna Akhmatova, so was Marina Tsvetaeva. They would have become what they became even if none of the historical events that befell Russia in this century had taken place: because they were *gifted*. Basically, talent doesn't need history.

Would Nadezhda Mandelstam have become what she became had it not been for the revolution and all the rest that followed? Probably not, for she met her future husband in 1919. But the question itself is immaterial; it leads us into the murky domains of the law of probability and of historical determinism. After all, she became what she became not because of what took place in Russia in this century but rather in spite of it. A casuist's finger will surely point out that from the point of view of historical determinism "in spite of" is synonymous with "because." So much then for historical determinism, if it gets so mindful about the semantics of some human "in spite of."

For a good reason, though. For a frail woman of sixty-five turns out to be capable of slowing down, if not averting in the long run, the cultural disintegration of a whole nation. Her memoirs are something more than a testimony of her times; it's the view of history in the light of conscience and culture. In that light history winces, and an individual realizes his choice: between seeking that light's source and committing an anthropological crime against himself.

She didn't mean to be so grand, nor did she simply try to get even with the system. For her it was a private matter, a matter of her temperament, of her identity and what had shaped that identity. As it were, her identity had been shaped by culture, by its best products: her husband's poems. It's them, not his memory, that she was trying to keep alive. It's to them, and not to him, in the course of forty-two years that she became a widow. Of course she loved him, but love itself is the most elitist of passions. It acquires its stereoscopic substance and perspective only in the context of culture, for it takes up more place in the mind than it does in the bed. Outside of that setting it falls flat into one-dimensional friction. She was a widow to culture, and I think she loved her husband more at the end than on the day they got married. That is probably why readers of her books find them so haunting. Because of that, and because the status of the modern world vis-à-vis civilization also can be defined as widowhood.

If she lacked anything, it was humility. In that respect she was quite unlike her two poets. But then they had their art, and the quality of their achievements provided them with enough contentment to be, or to pretend to be, humble. She was terribly opinionated, categorical, cranky, disagreeable, idiosyncratic; many of her ideas were half-baked or developed on the basis of hearsay. In short, there was a great deal of one-upwomanship in her, which is not surprising given the size of the figures she was reckoning with in reality and later in imagination. In the end, her intolerance drove a lot of people away, but that was quite all right with her, because she was getting tired of adulation, of being liked by Robert McNamara and Willy Fisher (the real name of Colonel Rudolph Abel). All she wanted was to die in her bed, and, in a way, she looked forward to dying, because "up there I'll be again with Osip." "No," replied Akhmatova, upon hearing this. "You've got it all wrong. Up there it's now me who is going to be with Osip."

Her wish came true, and she has died in her bed. Not a small thing for a Russian of her generation. There undoubtedly will surface those who will cry that she misunderstood her epoch, that she lagged behind the train of history running into the future. Well, like nearly every other Russian of her generation, she learned only too well that that train running into the future stops at the concentration camp or at the gas chamber. She was lucky that she missed it, and we are lucky that she told us about its route. I saw her last on May 30, 1972, in that kitchen of hers, in Moscow. It was late afternoon, and she sat, smoking, in the corner, in the deep shadow cast by the tall cupboard onto the wall. The shadow was so deep that the only things one could make out were the faint flicker of her cigarette and the two piercing eyes. The rest—her smallish shrunken body under the shawl, her hands, the oval of her ashen face, her gray, ashlike hair—all were consumed by the dark. She looked like a remnant of a huge fire, like a small ember that burns if you touch it.

—March 5, 1981

I I

ARTHUR GOLD AND ROBERT FIZDALE
ON GEORGE BALANCHINE

There was a star danced, and under that was I born.
—*Much Ado About Nothing*

GEORGE BALANCHINE LIKED to say, quoting Mayakovsky, "I am not a man, but a cloud in trousers." And now the luminous cloud has floated off, leaving us with a loss far deeper than the grave. Balanchine spoke for all of us. Diffident as he was in private life, in his ballets he shared his daydreams, his joys, his troubled loves, his fears, his instinct for elegance and order, and his passion for youth with those who admired his work. He has been a poet for poets, a musician for musicians, and a dramatist for anyone who wishes to understand the human heart. Reality for him was the stage and he gave us stylized visions that seem truer than life. His genius was multilingual. A couple in love walk slowly onto a twilit stage, music of Fauré is heard, and the perfume of French poetry lies lightly in air. *The Four Temperaments* and *Kammermusik* speak perfect German. *Agon*— cool, sarcastic, analytic, probing—is Sixties America. Stravinsky said when he first saw *Movements for Piano and Orchestra*, "George shows me things in my own music that I didn't realize were there."

W. H. Auden said of Balanchine, "He's not an intellectual, he's something deeper, a man who understands everything." And indeed, he has given us a history of manners, music, and the dance, as seen by a twentieth-century master. Through his eyes we saw gods and mythical creatures move in limitless space. *Apollo* (and could this be the twenty-four-year-old Balanchine's youthful aspiration?) harnesses the muses and controls their destinies—controls them with godlike tact and tenderness. Balanchine's genius is unclassifiable. He can be a neoclassicist for Stravinsky, a romantic for Schumann's *Davidsbündlertänze* and Brahms's *Liebeslieder Walzer*. For Ravel he has been a classicist in *Le Tombeau de Couperin*, a Proustian in *Valse Noble et Sentimentale*, and an Edgar Allan Poe in *La Valse*. Delight, pleasure, and charm do not seem to be twentieth-century preoccupations until we see *Valse Fantaisie, Bourrée Fantasque, Square Dance*, or *Nutcracker* for that matter. Gothic romance as an art form was forgotten until *La Sonnambula*, whose quickly sketched *intrigante* plotting evil as she dances the polonaise is a masterpiece of characterization. In the same ballet, we are bewitched by the somnambulist as, candle in hand, she makes her way around the stage *en pointe*, blindly seeking her destiny.

Balanchine's genius in dance innovation was limitless. His revolutionary use of the elements of ballet—speed, balances, steps, lifts, gestures, partnering—made us see them anew. As with Mozart, his inventions came to us as inevitable extensions of his art. Creation was his life, inventiveness his toy. He could transform everyday life into an unexpected fete.

"We'll be late for the theater," we said one evening after an early dinner. "Let's find a taxi."

"No, no," he said, "subway much better." And like a mythical guide he made the dingy steps, the sinister train, the underground arrival at the State Theater a Tiepoloesque flight into heaven. Ordinary life seemed not to exist for George. Olympian in his simplicity, he cooked his Russian food, he ironed his own shirts, he planted flowers and trees, he trained his cat to jump—all with the concentration, the dispatch, the single-mindedness that he gave to his choreography.

If his work gave him trouble no one was aware of it. A religious believer, he trusted the immense talent God had given him. Balanchine never tried consciously to create a masterpiece. He made masterpieces by combining his unique knowledge of the dance and a profound emotional instinct with an absolute honesty about the music he was working with. His nose would quiver with characteristic disdain at the word "inspiration." But how he inspired others! He could transform the dancing of Tanaquil Le Clercq or Suzanne Farrell with the severest, gentlest love and make them dance like angels.

We who have known Balanchine for almost forty years never failed (when he had time for us) to ask his musical advice. The essentials—rhythm, tempo, phrasing, and structure—were what he spoke of. Whenever expressiveness was mentioned he would say, "That you find in the music." Then with his enigmatic smile he would add, "And if you're lucky, in here," pointing to his heart.

His musical gifts were extraordinary. He could play anything at sight. In the early days of the New York City Ballet he would occasionally slip into the orchestra pit, unannounced and largely unnoticed, and conduct one of his ballets. Especially impressive was his ability to transcribe, to make piano reductions of complicated orchestral scores—Webern or Schoenberg—in order to study them before beginning to choreograph. In the slow movement of *Concerto Barocco* the soaring lifts of the ballerina follow the rising arch of the melody while the corps de ballet mirrors the mounting intensity of the harmonic progression—a breathtaking example of Balanchine's ability to make one "see the music and hear the dance."

Balanchine's own theater is only a step away from Broadway, for which he worked, and which, with few exceptions, deals, like a shifty croupier, in false coin. Close as they are they seem planets apart. For in his theater Balanchine created a cultural haven for those who can say the word "beauty" without shame. His standards were chivalric and unrelenting. He demanded nothing from his audience, expected little understanding from them, was happy if they appreciated his pretty girls and pleased when they seemed to grasp the true spirit of his work. He had little use for "highfalutin" appreciations, and dreaded the search for hidden meanings in his ballets. Poetic and metaphysical insights seemed only to startle him. And unlike Diaghilev, he was bored by the rich and the powerful.

Balanchine married Tamara Geva, Alexandra Danilova, Vera Zorina, Maria Tallchief, and Tanaquil Le Clercq. Each in turn became his muse; each showed him new ways to perceive love, the human spirit, and the body in motion. There were two other marriages in Balanchine's life; each lasted about fifty years and changed the course of ballet history. One was his long association with Lincoln Kirstein, the young visionary who presented Balanchine to America with such foresight, imagination, and princely dedication. The other was his creative alliance with Igor Stravinsky. From his young days in Saint Petersburg to his later years in New York he was the composer's partner in art, the artist closest to the spirit of Stravinsky's work.

Balanchine's personality, his quiet, aristocratic ideals of behavior, moral and physical, affected everyone near him. At his private burial each of his dancers, his associates, and his friends was given a rose to add to those that lay on the grave. As we watched them, each in turn, step forward to place their roses on the coffin, it seemed to us that they shared a grace, distinction, and nobility that were Balanchine's own, and that there had never been, and never again would be, another choreographer of George Balanchine's stature.

—June 2, 1983

12

JOHN RICHARDSON
ON DOUGLAS COOPER

ONE POINT THAT Douglas Cooper, the controversial English art historian who died last year, would want his obituarist to emphasize is that he was *not* Australian. True, his antecedents had acquired a considerable fortune, not to speak of a baronetcy, down under, but they returned to England around the turn of the century; and they sold their Australian holdings, including much of the Woollahra section of Sydney, some years later. Given his father's lifelong possession of a British passport and his mother's Dorset lineage, Cooper understandably resented his countrymen's tendency to endow him with an erroneous—i.e., Australian—provenance. A very minor irritant, one might have thought. Unfortunately resentment made for paranoia; paranoia made for Anglophobia; and Anglophobia made for the outlandish accents, *outré* clothes, and preposterous manner that Cooper cultivated. Bear in mind, however, that many of his *idées fixes* only made sense if turned upside down, or seen in the light of willful provocation or perversity. Anglophobia was the only form of patriotism that Cooper could permit himself.

Cooper's importance for art history is that he was the first person to study and collect Cubist works with the reverence and scholarship hitherto reserved for the old masters. Cooper's education was somewhat random: Repton, which he loathed, and a year or so successively at Cambridge, Freiburg im Breisgau, and the Sorbonne. When he was twenty-one (1932), he came into £100,000. This enabled him to defy his Bouguereau-owning parents, who hoped to force him into diplomacy or the law, and become a scholar like his erudite uncle, Gerald Cooper, the musicologist and collector of Purcell manuscripts. To get the hang of the art world, Cooper did a brief stint as a dealer—in partnership with Freddy Mayor of London's Mayor Gallery—but he was not prepared to make the concessions that this *métier* demanded. Thenceforth he devoted all his energies to chronicling modern art (an edition of Van Gogh's letters to Emile Bernard, published under the pseudonym of Douglas Lord,[1] was his first contribution to scholarship), and to collecting Cubism.

Nothing if not systematic by nature, Cooper set aside a third of his inheritance for his collection; and with this he went to work charting the development of the four most important artists of the Cubist movement (Picasso, Braque, Gris, Léger) subject by subject (still life, figure, landscape), medium by medium, and year by year. Cooper was lucky in that his chosen field was still relatively untilled. Much of the cream of Cubism, which had been thrown on the market ten years earlier by the four forced sales in Paris of Kahnweiler's stock, was not only still available, but prices had hardly changed over the previous decade. Moreover, Cooper found he had very few serious rivals. Thanks to his fastidious eye, hard-headed scholarship, and sufficient means, he managed in less than ten years to put together a collection that was unique in scope and quality. The very few gaps—a major Braque figure composition (a necessary pendant to Picasso's *Homme à la clarinette* of 1911), a Picasso landscape of 1908–1909,

---

1. This pseudonym was inspired by Lord Alfred Douglas.

and a "rococo" still life of 1914—were more than made up for by Cooper's acquisition of such landmarks as the first recorded *papier collé* (Braque's *Nature morte avec compotier* of September 1912) and an incomparable group of Léger's *Contrastes de forme* (four paintings and several large gouaches bought from Léonce Rosenberg around 1935 for about £5 each).

In his initial phase as a collector Cooper was greatly helped by his friendship with the shadowy German *marchand amateur*, G. F. Reber. Reber had originally made a collection of major post-impressionist paintings, most of which he subsequently exchanged (except for Cézanne's *Garçon au gilet rouge*, later sold to Emil Bührle) with Paul Rosenberg for important works by the artists that Cooper was acquiring. In addition to Cooper the principal client for Reber's remarkable stock was a young Sudeten art historian, the late Ingeborg Eichmann, who was also in the market for great modern paintings. According to Cooper, Reber always hoped—in vain—that marriage might ultimately link the two collections that he had helped to form. When short of cash—a frequent occurrence—Reber would sell one or other of his protégés a Picasso or Braque he had kept back for himself. This is how Cooper acquired his greatest treasure, Picasso's *Trois masques* (1907)—the most important work of the "Negro" period left in private hands—but only after redeeming it from Geneva's municipal pawnshop.

On the outbreak of war Cooper characteristically chose to remain in Paris and join a French ambulance unit organized by a fellow *mécène*, Comte Etienne de Beaumont. When the Germans invaded, Cooper's valiant care for the wounded won him the Médaille Militaire. He subsequently recounted his adventures in a book, *The Road to Bordeaux* (written with Denys Freeman), part of which was reissued by the Ministry of Information as a pamphlet against panic. On disembarking in England, Cooper—who had a lifelong horror of passing unperceived—contrived to get himself jailed (the loathsome English again!), for no better reason, he claimed, than that he was wearing a French uniform. Thanks to the intervention of a former minister of air, Cooper was rescued and commissioned in the intelligence service of the Royal Air Force. Given linguistic abilities that included a mimetic command of German—*Hochdeutsch* to *Wienerisch*—Cooper proved to be a demon interrogator of prisoners of war during the North African campaign, but the nervous strain was considerable, so was the toll on his psyche.

After a further spell of intelligence work in Malta at the height of the siege, Cooper was transferred to the Monuments and Fine Arts Branch, Control Commission for Germany. Once again his knowledge of the German language and character proved invaluable, and he briefly found fulfillment in passionate pursuit of Nazi art thieves and the dealers who had collaborated with them. He was especially proud of the hornet's nest he stirred up when he discovered the reason why Herr Montag—one of Hitler's leading looters—kept eluding his Vautrin-like grasp; Montag owed his liberty to having taught Churchill how to paint. One of the byproducts of Cooper's work for the commission was a small collection of fine works by Paul Klee, which he made in the course of investigative visits to Switzerland.

Back in London, Cooper moved in with his old friend, Lord Amulree, hung as much of the collection as the walls of 18 Egerton Terrace would hold, and embarked on a career of *Kunstwissenschaft* punctuated by controversy. The articles on nineteenth-and twentieth-century art that poured from his pen were at their best trenchant and innovative; at their worst, petty and spiteful—sometimes all these contradictory things at the same time. For instance, Cooper's catalog of the Courtauld collection abounds in original ideas (some of them Benedict Nicolson's), but his searching analysis of the impact that Impressionism had on English art and collecting was so marred in its original draft by attacks on Roger Fry that the chancellor of London University (the book's sponsor) was moved to ask if Fry had made off with Cooper's wife. And despite many remarkable contributions to *The Times Literary Supplement* (thoughtful essays on Ingres and Fénéon in particular), Cooper too often used the anonymity of the journal as cover from which to snipe on friend and foe alike, castigating them in interminable *sottisiers* for misplaced accents and typos rather than more heinous shortcomings. All the same his bitchy brilliance, his abrasiveness, his passionate and pugnacious outbursts were far more stimulating and enlightening than the Bloomsbury prissiness of his immediate predecessors: Roger Fry's halfhearted views on Cézanne or the vacuousness of Clive Bell's concept of significant form.

No wonder the Bloomsbury eunuchs fought shy of him, as did cautious Kenneth Clark and the British art establishment, and vice versa. No wonder official recognition failed to materialize. And no wonder he decided "to get the hell out." For a time he thought seriously about moving to New York, but given the extent to which his admiration for American collectors and scholars (the Muscum of Modern Art and its then director, Alfred Barr, in particular) was tinged with envy and sour grapes, it is as well that he never pursued this idea. Over the years, however, he made recurrent visits to these shores and derived intense pleasure from finding fault with any manifestations of connoisseurship that rivaled his own. Instead Cooper decided to emigrate to France. When he (and the present writer) discovered an abandoned folly, the colonnaded Château de Castille, for sale in the depths of Provence, he lost no time in moving—lock, stock, and paintings—to the country he had always preferred to England.

By the summer of 1950, the château was habitable, and for the first time Cooper's collection could be seen in its plenitude. Since there was no comparable conspectus of Cubist art in France—public or private—Castille soon became a pilgrimage place for anyone interested in the subject. After *L'Oeil* magazine published an article on *le château des cubistes*, the trickle of pilgrims grew to a stream—art historians, dealers, and American tourists poured through the house. Cooper basked in their interest and adulation, which he repaid with a fund of wit and good counsel. But what he most enjoyed was visits from the artists whose work was represented on his walls. Léger came for his second honeymoon, but Picasso was the most assiduous guest, so much so that Cooper saw himself in some respects as replacing Gertrude Stein in the artist's life.

Besides giving Cooper countless drawings (including a major study for the *Demoiselles d'Avignon*, later bequeathed to the Kunstmuseum, Basel), Picasso made a series of maquettes for the great murals (carried out in sandblasted cement by Karl Nesjar) in the former *magnanerie* at Castille. These decorations are still *in situ*, unlike Léger's vast *Circus* painting—executed (largely by assistants) for the château's staircase—which is now in the National Gallery of Australia. Besides artist, students were always especially welcome; however, given the split in Cooper's personality—it was as if an angel and a demon child were perpetually fighting for control—there was always the risk, indeed the probability, that the chatelain's solicitude and hospitality would change abruptly into irrational ire.

From his Provençal stronghold Cooper continued to collect—later works by former Cubists for the most part—and he made all manner of contributions to modern art history. He proved to be a most effective organizer of exhibitions, remorselessly browbeating artists, collectors, dealers, and institutions, the world over, into making loans (seldom reciprocated) to a succession of pathfinding shows: Monet and Braque in London and Edinburgh, Picasso in Marseille and Arles, Braque in Chicago, "The Cubist Epoch" in Los Angeles and New

York—to name but a few. He wrote books on Picasso, Léger, and de Staël. Although these do not always live up to the great expectations that his pontifical putdowns of rival authorities entitled us to expect, they present the complex processes of modern art in painfully sharp focus, very occasionally obscured by a clumsy thumb in front of the lens. In addition, historians will always be in Cooper's debt, given all the firsthand information that the former interrogator managed to wheedle out of his subjects. Too bad that he never produced the definitive work on Cubism or Picasso that he was uniquely qualified to write.

Slade Professor at Oxford in 1957–1958, visiting professor at Bryn Mawr in 1961, Cooper was also a tireless lecturer—in French, German, and Texan as well as his own tongue. But he never outgrew his penchant for controversy, as witness countless reviews of books and exhibitions whose aim was more to shock than to instruct. Alas, even when he was in the right, as he often was, Cooper would press his case to such vituperative lengths that he would consolidate the targets of his wrath in their job, opinions, or reputation, rather than the other way round. A case in point was "The Tate Affair"—a campaign by some of the more progressive trustees and staff members of the Tate Gallery to have the government remove an inept and reactionary director—which wasted much of his time and energy in the mid-Fifties. This business was the more regrettable in that it not only failed to right a wrong, but put Cooper under an unfortunate obligation to his comrade-in-arms, Graham Sutherland, the foremost British painter of the day.

An implicit quid pro quo for Sutherland's resignation as a Tate Gallery trustee—the move that triggered a protracted battle in the Treasury and the House of Commons—was that Cooper should write a monograph on the artist. The faint praise that materialized did little credit to the author or his subject. As Cooper later confessed, "a taste for Sutherland was incompatible with a taste for Cubism." He should have resisted, he said, the pressure to accord a minor British painter the accolade he had hitherto reserved for "the giants" of the Paris school. Cooper's much publicized fight with Sutherland, many years later, was an inevitable outcome of the false position in which the author found himself vis-à-vis the artist. In the circumstances it is a wonder that the portrait commemorating this ill-starred friendship escaped destruction. Cooper frequently threatened to follow the example of Lady Churchill, who consigned Sutherland's official portrait of her husband to the furnace, but he always allowed himself to be dissuaded from doing so.

After thieves broke into Castille in 1974 and made off with some of the smaller works (yet to be recovered), Cooper decided to sell the château and move somewhere safer and less remote. In 1977 he acquired what he described as "a bunker," a couple of small apartments in a modern building overlooking the sea in Monte Carlo. Since space was limited, he sold some of his larger paintings (including Picasso's *Homme à la clarinette*, now in the Thyssen-Bornemisza collection). However, even in its reduced form the collection retained its historical integrity; and enough fine things remained—indeed still remain in the hands of the collector's adopted son, William McCarty Cooper—to constitute a monument to the Cubist movement and the collector's discrimination. In Cooper's later years a self-destructive taste for feuding (he even managed to quarrel with his hero, Picasso), combined with failing health, condemned him to a relatively reclusive life. This was a good thing in that it enabled him to concentrate on such serious tasks as putting the finishing touches to the Juan Gris *catalogue raisonné*, on which he had been working for forty years, and to complete an as yet unpublished catalog of Gauguin's *oeuvre*.

Did Cooper, one wonders, come to have second thoughts about his native land? The last major exhibition he organized (with Gary

Tinterow), "Essential Cubism" (1983), at the Tate Gallery, consti-
tuted something of a rapprochement with England. This and the loan
of his Braque *Atelier* led the Tate to believe that the hatchet had been
buried. However the collector's fickle old heart had found yet another object, the Prado. And the pride of Cooper's last years was that
he was the first foreigner to become a member of that museum's *pa-
tronato*. In gratitude he gave the Prado a masterpiece by a Spanish
master virtually unrepresented in Spain: Juan Gris's portrait of his
wife. He also left the Prado his no less important *Nature morte aux
pigeons* (1912) by Picasso and the palette that this artist had used
while working on his *Déjeuner sur l'herbe* versions.

Cooper had started his career as a rebel in the cause of Cubism; he
ended as a rebel without any cause at all except a loathing for contemporary art, as witness his much-publicized denunciation of the
Tate's acquisition of a work by Carl André. It is not hard to see how
this came about. His narrow view of Cubism as the only valid yard-
stick by which to judge the art of this century doomed Cooper to
regard virtually everything done by post-Cubist artists, above all
nonfigurative ones, as a perversion or a *dégringolade*. In line with his
old-fogeyism, he adopted an apoplectic manner and took to dressing
up as one of his horsy forebears, only in *m'as tu vu* color schemes.
Like Evelyn Waugh in old age, he relished the role of sacred clown,
and cherished the belief that everyone was out of step but himself. As
Cooper was often in considerable pain, the clowning must have taken
a lot of courage to sustain, but his alternately fiendish and childish
wit never failed him. His end was in character. "I propose to die on
April Fool's Day," he announced as he went into the hospital for the
last time. And after three days in a coma, that is exactly what this
clown of genius did.

—April 25, 1985

13

HECTOR BIANCIOTTI
ON JORGE LUIS BORGES

TOWARD THE END of 1985 Borges had to undergo a series of medical examinations in Buenos Aires. He did not feel well; day by day the ground became less firm beneath his feet. This did not stop him from going to Geneva for the holidays—he wanted to spend them in the city of his adolescence. In mid-January he was taken to a hospital where, after suffering a hemorrhage, he had to submit to painful medical tests. I visited him there. We chatted, as if we were carrying on a dialogue from the night before, in bits and pieces. He talked of an old friend of Samuel Johnson who published a book under the title *The Joys of Madness*, and of Cocteau, whom he liked, at least partly, and he recited one of his poems to me. He told me that for some time the luminous fog that covered over his vision had turned violet, a color he detested. Then he described in detail the preface he had started to write—the night before, in the hospital—for the Pléiade edition of his work.

It was clear to me that his condition was grave. I remembered that he liked to cite the example of Socrates on his last day, when he refused to talk of death and went on discussing ideas with his friends, not wanting to make pathetic statements of farewell; he sent away his wife and children and nearly dismissed a friend who cried, because he wanted to talk in peace—simply talk, continue to think.

Borges would not express even the usual irritation at being in hospital. He made jokes about the food they gave him—soups and purées whose tastes were indefinable. "It could," he said, "be made of silk, of marble, of an extract of clouds." He was animated by this conversation, and Maria Kodama and I asked him if he would get up and walk with us in the corridor. Not without some fears, he accepted. At first trembling, he finished by holding himself straight and firm. He smiled, and in a voice that was weak but that became heavy and jarring and strong when he recited Anglo-Saxon or Icelandic texts, he chanted—one might say "intoned"—the last verse of the ballad of Maldon, just as we were leaving the corridor.

He released his beloved falcon into the forest
and entered the battle.

Two weeks later, he was back at his hotel. He could have returned to his house in Buenos Aires. He had reasons to do so; he feared what would happen to his old editions of Anglo-Saxon sagas. He decided to stay in Geneva, the city of his youth; he wanted to be near the lake. He worked to the end on a scenario for a film on Venice. He was glad to have visitors, always happy to talk to people capable of carrying on a dialogue with his vast memory and of contributing something unexpected to it.

One day he surprised me by asking me to bring him the works of Molière, the *Poèmes barbares* of Leconte de Lisle, and Michelet's *La Mer*. And then a few days later, the entire work of Remy de Gourmont, whom, he told me a little later, he thought of as his elder brother. "It's very unfair that he should be forgotten while I'm famous." In the evening the nurse read to him from Voltaire: "The best

French prose, perhaps the best prose ever written."

During the last months, he had two great wishes: first, to marry Maria Kodama, his student, his accomplice in the study of Anglo-Saxon and Icelandic literature, his fervent and attentive companion, his Antigone and his scribe—and he married her. Aside from this, he wanted to live in the old quarter of Geneva he had known when he was young, and the unfindable was found for him: an apartment on a very quiet *place*, where he could hear from time to time the sounds of nearby bells. As if he had the innocent power of great poets to transform reality and somehow make it resemble their own, the narrow little street on which the building stood had no name and no number at the door. There he felt at home, arrived, finally, at the center of the labyrinth. His happiness was so intense that the inextricable pattern that his steps, as he put it, had worn down (*"fatigué"*) for nearly eighty-seven years, now disappeared and, liberated, he could make his own way to the clouds.

When he was a student in Geneva, where the writer in him was born, a friend told him he must have some visiting cards. Borges's idea of what should appear on them as his "profession" could not have been more modest: *"Jorge Luis Borges, contemporain."* And now we have had the great luck to have been his contemporaries.

—August 14, 1986

14

GORE VIDAL
ON DAWN POWELL

ONCE UPON A time, New York City was as delightful a place to live in
as to visit. There were many amenities, as they say in brochures. One
was something called Broadway, where dozens of plays opened each
season, and thousands of people came to see them in an area which
today resembles downtown Calcutta without, alas, that subcontinen-
tal city's deltine charm and intellectual rigor.

One evening back there in once upon a time (February 7, 1957, to
be exact) my first play opened at the Booth Theatre. Traditionally,
the playwright was invisible to the audience: one hid out in a nearby
bar, listening to the sweet nasalities of Pat Boone's "Love Letters in
the Sand" from a glowing jukebox. But when the curtain fell on this
particular night, I went into the crowded lobby to collect someone.
Overcoat collar high about my face, I moved invisibly through the
crowd, or so I thought. Suddenly a voice boomed–tolled across the
lobby. "*Gore!*" I stopped; everyone stopped. From the cloakroom, a
small round figure, rather like a Civil War cannon ball, hurtled toward me and collided. As I looked down into that familiar round face
with its snub nose and shining bloodshot eyes, I heard, the entire
crowded lobby heard: "*How could you do this?* How could you *sell
out* like this? To *Broadway!* To *Commercialism!* How could you give

up *The Novel?* Give up the *security*. The security of knowing that every two years, there will be—like clockwork—*that five hundred dollar advance*!" Thirty years later, the voice still echoes in my mind, and I think fondly of its owner, our best comic novelist. "The field," I can hear Dawn Powell snarl, "is not exactly overcrowded."

On the night that *Visit to a Small Planet* opened, Dawn Powell was fifty-nine years old. She had published fourteen novels, evenly divided between accounts of her native Midwest (and how the hell to get out of there and make it to New York) and the highly comic New York novels, centered on Greenwich Village, where she lived most of her adult life. Some twenty-three years earlier, the Theater Guild had produced Powell's comedy *Jig Saw* (one of *her* many unsuccessful attempts to sell out to Commercialism) but there was third act trouble and despite Spring Byington and Ernest Truex, the play closed after forty-nine performances.

For decades Dawn Powell was always just on the verge of ceasing to be a cult and becoming a major religion. But despite the work of such dedicated cultists as Edmund Wilson and Matthew Josephson, John Dos Passos and Ernest Hemingway, Dawn Powell never became the popular writer that she ought to have been. In those days, with a bit of luck, a good writer eventually attracted voluntary readers, and became popular. Today, of course, "popular" means bad writing that is widely read while good writing is that which is taught to involuntary readers. Powell failed on both counts. She needs no interpretation while in her lifetime she should have been as widely read as, say, Hemingway or the early Fitzgerald or the mid O'Hara or even the late, far too late, Katherine Anne Porter. But Powell was that unthinkable monster, a witty woman who felt no obligation to make a single, much less final, down payment on Love or The Family; she saw life with a bright Petronian neutrality, and every host at life's feast was a potential Trimalchio to be sent up.

In the few interviews that Powell gave, she often mentions, surprisingly for an American, much less a woman of her time and place, *The Satyricon* as her favorite novel. This sort of thing was not acceptable then any more than it is now. Descriptions of warm mature heterosexual love were—and are—woman's writerly task, and the truly serious writers really, heart-breakingly, flunk the course while the pop ones pass with bright honors. Although Powell received very little serious critical attention (to the extent that there has ever been much in our heavily moralizing culture), when she did get reviewed by a really serious person like Diana Trilling (*The Nation*, May 29, 1948), La Trilling warns us that the book at hand is no good because of "the discrepancy between the power of mind revealed on every page of her novel [*The Locusts Have No King*] and the insignificance of the human beings upon which she directs her excellent intelligence." Trilling does acknowledge the formidable intelligence but because Powell does not deal with Morally Complex People (full professors at Columbia in mid journey?), "the novel as a whole ... fails to sustain the excitement promised by its best moments."

Apparently, a novel to be serious must be about very serious even solemn people rendered in a very solemn even serious manner. Wit? What is that? But then we all know that power of mind and intelligence count for as little in the American novel as they do in American life. Fortunately neither appears with sufficient regularity to distress our solemn middle-class middlebrows as they trudge ever onward to some Scarsdale of the mind, where the red light blinks and blinks at pier's end and the fields of the republic rush forward ever faster like a rug rolling up.

Powell herself occasionally betrays bewilderment at the misreading of her work. She is aware, of course, that the American novel is a middlebrow middle-class affair and that the reader/writer must be as one in pompous self-regard. "There is so great a premium on dullness," she wrote sadly (Robert van Gelder, *Writers and Writing*, Scribner's, 1946), "that it seems stupid to pass it up." She also remarks that

> it is considered jolly and good-humored to point out the oddities of the poor or of the rich. The frailties of millionaires or garbage collectors can be made to seem amusing to persons who are not millionaires or garbage collectors. Their ways of speech, their personal habits, the peculiarities of their thinking are considered fair game. I go outside the rules with my stuff because I can't help believing that the middle class is funny, too.

Well, she was warned by four decades of book chatterers.

My favorite was the considered judgment of one Frederic Morton (*The New York Times*, September 12, 1954):

> But what appears most fundamentally lacking is the sense of outrage which serves as an engine to even the most sophisticated [*sic*] satirist. Miss Powell does not possess the pure indignation that moves Evelyn Waugh to his absurdities and forced Orwell into his haunting contortions. Her verbal equipment is probably unsurpassed among writers of her genre—but she views the antics of humanity with too surgical a calm.

It should be noted that Mr. Morton was the author of the powerful, purely indignant, and phenomenally compassionate novel, *Asphalt and Desire*. In general, Powell's books usually excited this sort of commentary (Waugh *indignant*? Orwell hauntingly *contorted*?). The fact is that Americans have never been able to deal with wit. Wit gives away the scam. Wit blows the cool of those who are forever expressing a sense of hoked-up outrage. Wit, deployed by a woman with surgical calm, is a brutal assault upon nature—that is, Man. Attis, take arms!

Finally, as the shadows lengthened across the greensward, Edmund Wilson got around to his old friend (November 17, 1962) in *The New Yorker*. One reason, he tells us, why Powell has so little appeal to those Americans who read novels is that: "She does nothing to stimulate feminine day-dreams [Sexist times!]. The woman reader can find no comfort in identifying herself with Miss Powell's heroines. The women who appear in her stories are likely to be as sordid and absurd as the men." This sexual parity was—is—unusual. But now, closer to century's end than 1962, Powell's sordid, absurd ladies seem like so many Mmes. de Stael compared to our latter-day viragos.

Wilson also noted Powell's originality: "Love is not Miss Powell's theme. Her real theme is the provincial in New York who has come on from the Middle West and acclimatized himself (or herself) to the city and made himself a permanent place there, without ever, however, losing his fascinated sense of an alien and anarchic society." This is very much to the (very badly written) point. Wilson finds her novels "among the most amusing being written, and in this respect quite on a level with those of Anthony Powell, Evelyn Waugh, and Muriel Spark." Wilson's review was of her last book, *The Golden Spur*; three years later she was dead of breast cancer. "Thanks a lot, Bunny," one can hear her mutter as this belated floral wreath came flying through her transom.

* * *

Summer, Sunday afternoon. Circa 1950. Dawn Powell's duplex living room at 35 East Ninth Street. The hostess presides over an elliptical aquarium filled with gin: a popular drink of the period known as the martini. In attendance, Coby—just Coby to me for years, her *cavalier servente*; he is neatly turned out in a blue blazer; rosy-faced; sleek silver hair combed straight back. Coby can talk with charm on any subject. The fact that he might be Dawn's lover has never crossed my mind. They are so old. A handsome young poet lies on the floor, literally at the feet of E. E. Cummings and his wife Marion, who ignore him. Dawn casts an occasional maternal eye in the boy's direction; but the eye is more that of the mother of a cat or a dog, apt to make a nuisance. Conversation flows. Gin flows. Marion Cummings is beautiful; so indeed is her husband, his eyes a faded denim blue. Coby is in great form. Though often his own subject, he records not boring triumphs but improbable disasters. He is always broke, and a once distinguished wardrobe is now in the hands of those gay receivers, his landladies. On this afternoon, at home, Dawn is demure; thoughtful. "Why," she suddenly asks, eyes on the long body beside the coffee table, "do they never have floors of their own to sleep on?"

Cummings explains that since the poet lives in Philadelphia he is too far from his own floor to sleep on it. Not long after, the young poet and I paid a call on the Cummingses. We were greeted at the door by an edgy Marion. "I'm afraid you can't come in." Behind her an unearthly high scream sounded. "Dylan Thomas just died," she explained. "Is that Mr. Cummings screaming?" asked the poet politely, as the keening began on an even higher note. "No," said Marion. "That is not Mr. Cummings. That is Mrs. Thomas."

But for the moment, in my memory, the poet is forever asleep on the floor while on a balcony high up in the second story of Dawn's living room, a gray blurred figure appears and stares down at us. "Who," I ask, "is that?"

Dawn gently, lovingly, stirs the martinis; squints her eyes; says, "My husband, I think. It is Joe, isn't it, Coby?" She turns to Coby, who beams and waves at the gray man, who withdraws. "Of course it is," says Coby. "Looking very fit." I realize, at last, that this is a *ménage à trois* in Greenwich Village. My martini runs over.

—November 5, 1987

15

BRUCE CHATWIN
ON GEORGE ORTIZ

For Olivier on his 21st birthday

OLIVIER, YOUR FATHER and I have known each other since I was eighteen and he was thirty-one and I always associate him with hilarious moments. None was more hilarious than our visit to the Soviet Union which coincided with your arrival.

You will have been told a thousand times how your great-grandfather was a Bolivian *hacendero*, who, one day, found two American trespassers with bags of mineral specimens on their backs. He locked them in a stable, thinking the minerals might be gold or silver. Finally they confessed the specimens were tin. That is one side of your family history.

In the spring, twenty-one years ago, your father learned that I had an official invitation to visit archaeological museums in the Soviet Union and also to meet Soviet archaeologists. The man who invited me I had met the year before in Sofia where I assured him that a treasury supposed to have been found at Troy, was either a fake or a fake on paper. The rest of the party was to include my professor of archaeology and a lady Marxist archaeological student from Hampstead.

We met in Leningrad. G.O. was Doctor O of the Basel Museum.

For the first days he behaved like Dr. O. He listened patiently—although he nearly exploded afterward—to the rantings of an orthodox Marxist archaeologist. The museum impressed him greatly. He saw Greek objects, but he saw objects he had never seen before, treasures from the frozen tombs of Siberia, objects from the Siberian taiga.

On our last day in Leningrad we had an interview with the deputy director of the Hermitage Museum. The director himself was away in Armenia excavating the site of Urartu. It would not be fair to say that your father reached the door handle, but he is not a tall man, and the space suited him ideally. We were, after all, in the Tsar's reception room. The deputy director greeted us with great kindness, but was plainly quite shocked by his previous visitor. As we entered a notorious peddler of fakes from Madison Avenue went out. He had told the deputy director, in the name of his own foundation for the investigation of forgeries, that the celebrated Peter the Great Gold Treasure had been made by a jeweler in Odessa in 1898. Your father rose to the occasion and assured the man that his visitor had been a complete fraud. He then got carried away. The mask of Dr. O vanished. He said, "This is the greatest museum in the world, right? I am the greatest collector of Greek bronzes in the world. If I leave you my collection in my will, will you appoint me director of this museum for a number of years?"

We went on to Moscow and stayed at the Metropol Hotel. Dr. O reasserted his identity. Again, in the Russian Historical Museum, he saw objects he had never dreamed of. We went to a reception to meet seventy Soviet scholars and had to stand in line having our hands crushed. Our host, the top archaeologist of the Soviet Union and my friend from Sofia, was there to greet us. By the window, G.O. and I saw a pair of very cheerful figures looking at us with amusement. I said, "One is an Armenian, the other a Georgian." When our fingers stopped being crushed, we went over to these two gentlemen. I was right about the Armenian. The other, with a huge black mustache, was a Greek from Central Asia. I asked what they were laughing about. They said they had just been paid for their doctoral thesis and were deciding if they had enough money to go to the Moscow food market and buy a whole sheep for a barbeque.

G.O. passed the test of being a great Greek scholar. On our last evening in Moscow we were invited by the top archaeologist himself to an Uzbeg banquet. The only dish was a lamb stuffed with rice, apricots, and spices. The whole party became extremely drunk on wine, on champagne, and, worst of all, on brandy. I was very drunk myself, but threw every second glass on to the floor. The Soviet academicians went under the table one by one. G.O., the Marxist lady archaeologist, and the professor went off to the lavatory and were sick. The top archaeologist, in a steel gray suit, was drunk and the only survivor except for his sister with whom he lived, and who did not drink. She asked me to recite speeches from Shakespeare. I stood up:

"If music be the food of love, play on,
Give me excess of it; that surfeiting,
The appetite may sicken, and so die.
That strain again, it had a dying fall;
O, it came o'er my ear like the sweet sound
That breathes upon a bank of violets."

* * *

"The quality of mercy is not strain'd . . ."

* * *

"I come to wive it wealthily in Padua;
If wealthily, then happily in Padua."

* * *

"Once more unto the breach, dear friends, once more;
Or close the wall up with our English dead.
In peace there's nothing so becomes a man
As modest stillness and humility;
But when the blast of war blows in our ears
Then summon up the action of a tiger;
Stiffen the sinews, summon up the blood,
Disguise fair nature with hard-favor'd rage."

The top archaeologist finally went under the table like a gray sea lion who could stand the open air no longer. It was time to go. The Western party had revived. I was still very drunk.

In Moscow it was the time of white nights. A large Volga limousine taxi appeared to be waiting for us. We drove back to the hotel. I lay down on the bed, which was furthest from the bathroom. "You were wonderful," said your father. "You showed them what Englishmen are made of."

"Look, I'm going to be sick. Get the woman to bring a basin."

"Now I know why England won the war."

"Get me a basin, quickly!"

"Do you think I should send my son to Eton?"

"Watch out," I cried—and a column of vomit fell diagonally across his bed.

"Look what you've done to my Charvet dressing-gown!"

I think this was the end of the Soviet Union for your father. He survived a day in Kiev but his thoughts were on Catherine and your birth. I feel I should record this on paper and offer it to you as a twenty-first birthday present.

—September 28, 1989

16

PHILIP ROTH
ON IVAN KLÍMA

BORN IN PRAGUE in 1931, Ivan Klíma has undergone what Jan Kott calls a "European education": during his adult years as a novelist, critic, and playwright his work was suppressed in Czechoslovakia by the Communist authorities (and his family members harried and punished right along with him), while during his early years, as a Jewish child, he was transported, with his parents, to the Terezin concentration camp by the Nazis. In 1969, when the Russians moved into Czechoslovakia, he was out of the country, in London, on the way to the University of Michigan to see a production of one of his plays and to teach literature. When his teaching duties ended in Ann Arbor in the spring of 1970, he returned to Czechoslovakia with his wife and two children to become one of the "admirable handful"—as a professor, recently reinstated at Charles University, described Klíma and his circle to me at lunch one day—whose persistent opposition to the regime made their daily lives extremely hard.

Of his fifteen or so novels and collections of stories, those written after 1970 were published openly only abroad, in Europe primarily; only two books—neither of them among his best—have appeared in America, where his work is virtually unknown. Coincidentally, Ivan Klíma's novel *Love and Garbage*, inspired in part by his months during the Seventies as a Prague street cleaner, was published in Czechoslovakia on the very day that I flew there to see him. He arrived at the airport to pick me up on February 22, after spending the morning in a Prague bookstore where readers who had just bought his book waited for him to sign their copies in a line that stretched from the shop into the street. (During my week in Prague, the longest lines I saw were for ice cream and for books.) The initial printing of *Love and Garbage*, his first Czech publication in twenty years, was 100,000 copies. Later in the afternoon, he learned that a second book of his, *My Merry Mornings*, a collection of stories, had been published that day as well, also in an edition of 100,000. In the three months since censorship has been abolished, a stage play of his has been produced and a TV play has been broadcast. Five more of his books are to appear this year.

Love and Garbage is the story of a well-known, banned Czech writer "hemmed in by prohibition" and at work as a street cleaner, who, for a number of years, finds some freedom from the claustrophobic refuge of his home—from the trusting wife who wants to make people happy and is writing a study on self-sacrifice; from the two dearly loved growing children—with a moody, spooky, demanding sculptress, a married mother herself, who comes eventually to curse him and to slander the wife he can't leave. To this woman he is erotically addicted.

> There was a lot of snow that winter. She'd take her little girl to her piano lessons. I'd walk behind them, without the child being aware of me. I'd sink into the freshly fallen snow because I wasn't looking where I was going, I was watching her walking....

It is the story of a responsible man who guiltily yearns to turn his back on all the bitter injustices and to escape into a "private region of bliss." "My ceaseless escapes" is how he reproachfully describes the figure in his carpet.

At the same time, the book is a patchwork rumination on Kafka's spirit (the writer mentally works up an essay about Kafka while he's out cleaning streets), on the meaning of soot, smoke, filth, and garbage in a world which can turn even people into garbage, on death, on hope, on fathers and sons (a dark, tender leitmotif is the final illness of the writer's father), and, among other things, on the decline of Czech into "jerkish." Jerkish is the name of the language developed in the US some years back for the communication between people and chimpanzees; it consisted of 225 words and Klíma's hero predicts that, after what has happened to his own language under the Communists, it can't be long before jerkish is spoken by all of mankind. "Over breakfast," says this writer whom the state will not allow to be published, "I'd read a poem in the paper by the leading author writing in jerkish." The four banal little quatrains are quoted. "For this poem of 69 words," he says, "including the title, the author needed a mere 37 jerkish terms and no idea at all.... Anyone strong enough to read the poem attentively will realize that for a jerkish poet even a vocabulary of 225 words is needlessly large."

Love and Garbage is a wonderful book, marred only by some distressing lapses into philosophical banality that crop up particularly as the central story winds down and—in the English version just published by Chatto and Windus in London—by the translator's inability to imagine a pungent, credible demotic idiom appropriate to the argot of the social misfits in Klíma's street-cleaning detail. It is an inventive book that—aside from its absurdist title—is wholly unexhibitionistic. Klíma juggles a dozen motifs and undertakes the boldest transitions without hocus-pocus, as unshowily as Chekhov telling the story "Gooseberries"—he provides a nice antidote to all that magic in magic realism. The simplicity with which he creates his elaborate collage—harrowing concentration camp memories, ecological reflections, imaginary spats between the estranged lovers, and down-to-earth Kafkean analysis all juxtaposed and glued to the ordeal of the exhilarating, exhausting adultery—is continuous with the disarming directness, verging on adolescent ingenuousness, with which the patently autobiographical hero confesses his emotional turmoil.

The book is permeated by an intelligence whose tenderness colors everything and is unchecked and unguarded by irony. Klíma is, in this regard, Milan Kundera's antithesis—an observation that might seem superfluous were it not for an astounding correspondence of preoccupations. The temperamental divide between the two is considerable, their origins diverge as sharply as the paths they've taken as men, and yet their affinity for the erotically vulnerable, their struggle against political despair, their brooding over the social excreta, whether garbage or kitsch, a shared inclination for extended commentary and for mixing modes—not to mention their fixation on the fate of outcasts—create an odd, tense kinship, one not as unlikely as it might seem to both writers. I sometimes had the feeling while reading *Love and Garbage* that I was reading *The Unbearable Lightness of Being* turned inside out. The rhetorical contrast between the two titles indicates just how discordant, even adversarial, the perspectives can be of imaginations engaged similarly with similar themes—in this case, with what Klíma's hero calls "the most important of all themes, . . . suffering resulting from a life deprived of freedom."

During the early Seventies, when I began to make a trip to Prague each spring, Ivan Klíma was my principal reality instructor. In his car he drove me around to the street-corner kiosks where writers sold cigarettes, to the public buildings where they mopped the floors, to the construction sites where they were laying bricks, and out of the city to the municipal waterworks where they slogged about in overalls and boots, a wrench in one pocket and a book in the other. When I got to talk at length with these writers, it was often over dinner at Ivan's house.

After 1976 I was no longer able to get a visa to enter Czechoslovakia and we corresponded through the West German or Dutch couriers who discreetly carried mail, manuscripts, and books in and out of the country for the people who were under close surveillance. By the summer of 1978, ten years after the Russian invasion, even Ivan, who had always seemed to me the most effervescent of those I'd met in the opposition, was sufficiently exhausted to admit, in a letter written in somewhat uneven English, "Sometime I hesitate if it is reasonable to remain in this misery for the rest of our life." He went on:

> Our life here is not very encouraging—the abnormality lasts too long and is depressing. We are persecuted the whole time, it is not enough that we are not allowed to publish a single word in this country—we are asked for interrogations, many of my friends were arrested for the short time. I was not imprisoned, but I am deprived of my driving license (without any reason of course) and my telephone is disconnected. But what is the worst: one of our colleagues. . . .

Not uncharacteristically, he then described at much greater length a writer he considered to be in straits more dire than his own.

Fourteen years after I last saw him, Ivan Klíma's engaging blend of sprightliness and stolidness struck me as amazingly intact and his strength undiminished. Even though his Beatle haircut has been clipped back a bit since the Seventies, his big facial features and mouthful of large, carnivore teeth still make me sometimes think (particularly when he's having a good time) that I'm in the presence of a highly intellectually evolved Ringo Starr. Ivan had been at the center of the activities known now in Czechoslovakia as "the revolution," and yet he showed not the least sign of the exhaustion which even the young students reading English literature, whose Shakespeare class I sat in on at the university, told me had left them numb with fatigue and relieved to be back quietly studying even something as abstruse to them as the opening scenes of *Macbeth*.

I got a momentary reminder of the stubborn force in Klíma's temperament during dinner at his house one evening, while he was advising a writer friend of his and mine how to go about getting back the tiny two-room apartment that had been confiscated by the authorities in the late Seventies, when the friend had been hounded by the secret police into an impoverished exile. "Take your wife," Ivan told him, "take your four children, and go down to the office of Jaroslav Kořán." Jaroslav Kořán is the brand-new mayor of Prague, formerly a translator of poetry from English; as the week passed and I either met or heard about Havel's appointees, it began to seem to me as though a primary qualification for joining the new administration was having translated into Czech the poems of John Berryman. Have there ever before been so many translators, novelists, and poets at the head of anything other than the PEN club?

"In Kořán's office," Ivan continued, "lie down on the floor, all of you, and refuse to move. Tell them, 'I'm a writer, they took my apartment, and I want it back.' Don't beg, don't complain—just lie there and refuse to move. You'll have an apartment in twenty-four hours." The writer without an apartment—a very spiritual and mild person who, since I'd seen him last selling cigarettes in Prague, had aged in all the ways that Ivan had not—responded only with a forlorn smile suggesting, gently, that Ivan was out of his mind. Ivan turned to me and said, matter-of-factly, "Some people don't have the stomach for this."

Helena Klimová, Ivan's wife, is a psychotherapist who received her training in the underground university that the dissidents conducted in various living rooms during the Russian occupation. When I asked how her patients were responding to the revolution and the new society it had ushered in, she told me, in her precise, affable, serious way, "The psychotics are getting better and the neurotics are getting worse." "How do you explain that?" I asked. "With all this new freedom," she said, "the neurotics are terribly uncertain. What will happen now? Nobody knows. The old rigidity was detestable, even to them, of course, but also reassuring, dependable. There was a structure. You knew what to expect and what not to expect. You knew whom to trust and whom to hate. To the neurotics the change is very unsettling. They are suddenly in a world of choices." "And the psychotics? Is it really possible that they're getting better?" "I think so, yes. The psychotics suck up the prevailing mood. Now it's exhilaration. Everybody is happy, so the psychotics are even happier. They are euphoric. It's all very strange. Everybody is suffering from adaptation shock."

I asked Helena what she was herself having most difficulty adapting to. Without any hesitation she answered that it was all the people who were suddenly nice to her who never had been before—it wasn't that long ago that she and Ivan had been treated most warily by neighbors and associates looking to avoid trouble. Helena's expression of anger over the rapidity with which those once so meticulously cautious—or outright censorious—people were now adapting to the Klímas was a surprise to me, since when I had known her during their hardest years she had always impressed me as a marvel of tolerance and equilibrium. The psychotics were getting better, the neurotics were getting worse, and, despite the prevailing mood of exhilaration, among the bravely decent, the admirable handful, some were now beginning openly to seethe a little with those poisoned emotions whose prudent management fortitude and sanity had demanded during the decades of resistance.

On my first full day in Prague, before Ivan came to meet me to begin our talks, I went off for a morning walk on the shopping streets just off Václavské náměsti, the big open boulevard where the crowds that helped to chant the revolution through to success first assembled last November. In only a few minutes, outside a storefront, I encountered a loose gathering of some seventy or eighty people, laughing at a voice coming over a loudspeaker. From the posters and inscriptions on the building I saw that, unwittingly, I had found the headquarters of Civic Forum.

This crowd of shoppers, strollers, and office workers was standing around together listening—as best I could figure out—to a comedian who must have been performing in an auditorium inside. I don't understand Czech but I guessed that it was a comedian—and a very funny one—because the staccato rhythm of his monologue, the starts, stops, and shifts of tone, seemed consciously designed to provoke the crowd into spasms of laughter that ripened into a rich roar and culminated, at the height of their hilarity, with outbursts of applause. It sounded like the response you hear from the audience at a Chaplin movie. Just when I was ready to move on, I saw through a passageway that there was yet another laughing crowd of about the same size on the other side of the Civic Forum building. It was only when I crossed over to them that I understood what I was witnessing. On two television sets situated above the front window of Civic Forum was the comedian himself: viewed in close-up, seated alone at a conference table, was the former first secretary of the Czech Communist party, Miloš Jakeš. Jakeš, who'd been driven from office early in December, was addressing a closed meeting of Party apparatchiks in the industrial city of Pilsen in October 1989.

I knew that it was Jakeš at the Pilsen meeting because the evening before, at dinner, Ivan and his son, Michal, had told me all about this videotape, which had been made secretly by the staff of Czech TV.

Now it played continuously outside the Prague headquarters of Civic Forum, where passers-by stopped throughout the day to have a good laugh. What they were laughing at was Jakeš's dogmatic, humorless Party rhetoric and his primitive, awkward Czech—the deplorably entangled sentences, the ludicrous malapropisms, the euphemisms and evasions and lies, the pure jerkish, that, only months earlier, had filled so many people with shame and loathing. Michal had told me that on New Year's Eve Radio Free Europe had played Jakeš's Pilsen videotape as "the funniest performance of the year."

Watching people walk back out into the street grinning, I thought that this must be the highest purpose of laughter, its sacramental reason-for-being—to bury wickedness in ridicule. It seemed a very hopeful sign that so many ordinary men and women (and teen-agers, and even children, who were in the crowd) should be able to recognize that the offense against their language had been as humiliating and atrocious as anything else. Ivan told me later that at one point during the revolution, a vast crowd had been addressed for a few minutes by a sympathetic young emissary from the Hungarian democratic movement, who concluded his remarks by apologizing to them for his imperfect Czech. Instantaneously, as one voice, a half million people roared back, "You speak better than Jakeš."

Pasted to the window beneath the TV sets were two of the ubiquitous posters of the face of Havel, whose Czech is everything that Jakeš's is not.

—April 12, 1990

17

ELENA BONNER
ON ANDREI SAKHAROV

IT IS DIFFICULT for me to write about Andrei Dmitrievich Sakharov's *Memoirs*. I do not have the proper distance from the book, almost no distance at all. Nor do I have the strength to try to look at it from the outside. Every time I pick up the book, even simply touching the cover, I am pierced by the painful realization that Andrei did not see it. I feel myself inside the book, and I perceive it as a child that came into the world through my efforts and was nursed through its illnesses, saved from evil, and miraculously survived. It may seem that I am exaggerating. But I am speaking not of the actual work I did during the years when Sakharov was writing this book, but of my attitude toward it, so that the reader will understand that I cannot be objective about it.

Of course, I see that the book is written unevenly, sometimes it is a bit too abstract, too dry. The two chapters largely about physics might seem unnecessary to some, even though there probably wasn't a single day in the life of Andrei Dmitrievich when he didn't think about science, and there was a time when physics pushed everything else into the background. And sometimes I think the book lacks the explicit characterizations of certain people that I heard from him in our private conversations. But all that is made up for by the author's absolute honesty, from the first line to the last, in evaluating his own thoughts, decisions, and actions. This is not the typical neurotic introspection of a twentieth-century intellectual, but reflects an extraordinary ability to judge himself soberly and even calmly, as if he were seeing himself inside and out. And then there is his voice. I say voice even though I realize a book is not a record, but you can hear Andrei Dmitrievich's voice in the book. I am thrilled that several of his friends spoke to me specifically of his voice after they read it.

The author's foreword states that the book was begun in the summer of 1978, and the date at the end of the book is February 15, 1983. This is both true and not true. Early in our life together we agreed never to travel separately. But life decided otherwise. Since we had many enforced separations, Andrei decided to write a diary for me. In late December 1975, after I went to Italy for eye surgery and to Oslo, where I represented Andrei Dmitrievich Sakharov at the ceremony for the Nobel Peace Prize, I read the thick notebook with a dark blue cover which Andrei had filled up over those four months.

When I finished, I regretted that it was so short. That regret quickly grew into resentment that Andrei had not kept a diary as a teen-ager, a student, a young man—all his life. His first diary at the age of fifty-four! My resentment was not directed at anyone in particular, but I expressed it to him along with my gratitude. Now I can't even remember which I felt the more. But I do remember Andrei arguing in the late night commuter train (we were living in Novogireyevo on the outskirts of Moscow—or rather, just spending nights there, while our life went on in the crowded and cramped apartment on Chkalov Street) that when Leo Tolstoy and Dostoevsky write diaries they are of interest, but when anyone else does, he does so out of an inferiority complex. And Andrei used to say, whether seriously or jokingly, that he got rid of all his complexes in August 1971. However, there was something that he liked about the work, and he kept a diary during all our other separations and even sometimes when we were together.

He usually made his entries at night and then brought the notebook to bed for me to read. Sometimes he asked me to fill in the blanks. Once, when I was very sleepy, I said that it wasn't proper for him to give me his diary to read and that a diary is written for the writer alone, to which Andrei replied, "You are me." He had heard those words of the writer Yuri Olesha from me after he met Olesha's widow, Olga Suok, in Peredelkino, where I was renting a dacha for my mother and my son. That was still in the days when I called him Andrei Dmitrievich, even though he called me Lusia from our first meeting.

In 1977 we lived through a second lengthy separation. I was in Italy again, for a second eye operation in that country (my third altogether). When I got back, another fat blue notebook was waiting for me. This time as I read it I suddenly realized that it was pointless for me to regret the absence of diaries for the part of his life that Andrei spent without me. He simply had to write about it. For whom? The question never arose as far as I was concerned. I was sufficiently egocentric to assume that it would be just for me. And I presented the idea to Andrei in almost that form. He countered by saying he had no time and that if now I normally sat up at the typewriter until past midnight, I would be up all night if he started writing. But his main argument against a diary was that I knew it all anyway. I insisted that I could forget, like any other human being. He maintained that I had a good memory. I said that I could die before him and he might have forgotten everything by then because he could end up hopelessly senile. He insisted that he would die before me—at the age of seventy-two, the same age as his father at the time of his death. If he'd been right, he'd have had three more years, an eternity.

We argued about the book seriously and jokingly many times, but

I began to notice that Andrei was bringing it up himself, although from a different point of view: that I should write a book. Or he'd suggest writing one together. We would take the year 1935, for instance, and he would describe his life at the time and I would describe mine. And at the end of that chapter we would examine events from the standpoint of the theory of probability—why didn't we meet on Tverskoi Boulevard that year? Back then I called the idea both a layer cake and a double bed of collected works, even though now the idea doesn't seem as silly as it did then. The first definition was mine. The other I stole from Victor Shklovsky, who once referred in my presence in those terms to a joint work by Elsa Triolet and Louis Aragon. I replied that a double bed was a good thing, but a book has a different function. In that argument I recalled the words of the mother of one of my girl friends from school. It was in the days when people cooked on a Primus stove, which used kerosene (not everyone may know that now). She was dining at a friend's house and when she was asked how she liked the soup (into which some kerosene had spilled), she replied that she liked "the soup separately and the kerosene separately." My argument was that my life was of no interest to anyone, that it was hopelessly banal, while his was unique.

In one of these arguments I understood for the first time that if he wrote the book, it certainly would not be for me alone. It might be one of the most important things Andrei did. But by then it was clear that Andrei was fighting rear-guard battles. The arguments over whether to write this book lasted much longer than my arguments with him to write an open letter to Senator James Buckley, which gave birth to the book *My Country and the World*, and a very brief discussion with him about writing the open letter to Dr. Sidney Drell on nuclear weapons. Of course, in the case of the latter, the brevity of the discussion might have been a function of the difficulty of arguing: all the debates between us took place on paper, with our mouths shut. We were in Gorky, where we were "serviced" by what must have been an entire squad of the best "listeners" of the Soviet Union (not to be confused with Heroes of the Soviet Union, even though they might sometimes be one and the same, doing the now-popular time sharing).

The summer of 1978 was a little less busy than the previous one and Andrei started writing. By September he had written the first four chapters. One day I persuaded him to read it aloud, and I taped the first chapter. Later, when he was sent to Gorky, and I made my first trip to Leningrad, our friends there listened to the tape. In late October 1978 the manuscript and my typescript were stolen from the apartment on Chkalov Street. A few things of no value also disappeared—some other papers, an old jacket of Andrei's, Mother's robe. From that moment on a mystery plot began in parallel with the book's writing. I once saw an Italian movie called *Cops and Robbers*. But in our mystery story the police were also the thieves. And if anyone ever wants to make a movie out of it, the title should be *Robber Cops and the Author and His Wife*.

The KGB declared war on the book and we began our struggle to save it. When I would manage to get a part of the manuscript abroad I would tell Andrei not by silently writing this down, but by quoting a favorite World War II song: "Our cause is just, and the enemy will be destroyed." And when an attempt would fail, I'd quote another wartime song: "It's a people's war, a holy war. . . ." We joked about it, but sometimes we didn't feel like joking at all. When Andrei's bag, with his manuscript, diaries, and other documents, was stolen from the dentist's office, I was in Moscow. He met me at the train station the following morning. He looked gaunt and lost. His first words were "Lusia, they stole it." I didn't understand. "The bag," he said. He was so agitated that I thought the theft had taken place just then, right at the station. He seemed physically ill from the loss, and on the first day I did not argue with him when he said that he would stop writing, that we couldn't beat the KGB. But a day later I wrote on paper that he had to replace what was lost. Andrei did not write anything in response, but merely shook his head.

I blew up, forgetting all about the need for secrecy, and shouted that he was permitting the KGB to lead him around again and that as long as I was alive I wouldn't allow it. The word "again" was not an accident. At the very beginning of our life in Gorky our friend Natasha Gesse was allowed to visit. I left her there with Andrei and went to Moscow. While I was away, someone either from the KGB or the MVD named Glossen came and asked for Andrei's passport. Andrei looked through his papers, found it, and gave it to him. The next day he was called into the procurator's office and asked to sign an acknowledgment that he had been warned that my press conference in Moscow was a criminal action. He signed. It sometimes happened to him that he was so preoccupied with some thought or idea that he failed to react to what was being done to him. Besides, at the beginning of the Gorky period he felt that resisting the KGB was as pointless as resisting the weather.

When I got back, I threw a fit that made even Natasha, who usually defended him in everything, sit hunched up in a corner without uttering a single word. That was completely out of character for her. Of course her silence might have been caused by a feeling of guilt—after all, she had been there when this happened. Andrei immediately agreed with me. He sent the procurator's office a statement denying any significance to his signature. They returned the passport with a residency permit for Gorky, thereby making it seem as if his exile had some sort of legal basis.

Such stormy scenes occurred only a few other times in our life. Three of them happened after we had returned to Moscow. One was over a rally at the Academy of Sciences after his nomination to the

People's Congress had been blocked through the academy's chicanery, he was not elected. At the rally I moved aside when I saw that the TV cameras were about to film him and later had trouble making my way back through the crowd.

One of the demands and slogans of the rally was, "If not Sakharov, then whom?" I was certain that Andrei would get up on the tribunal and announce that he was withdrawing his candidacy in all the territorial districts where he had been nominated in order to support the rally's demand that he be on the academy's slate of nominees. I was astonished that he didn't do so.

On the way home in the car I said rather harshly that he was behaving almost like a traitor to the community of young scientists who were fighting not only for him but for other worthy people. That time Andrei did not agree with me immediately; but a few weeks later he reached the same conclusion and made a statement to the press. Of course, it would have been more elegant to have done it at the rally. (I use the word "elegant" in almost the same way Andrei did when describing a physics or mathematical solution as being elegant. He would say it slowly, savoring and enjoying the word.)

One of our arguments took place in the presence of several reporters, including Zhavoronkov from *Moscow News*. We were in a rush to catch a plane to Canada, and the reporter had come to persuade Andrei to repudiate our interview in *Le Figaro* with Jean-Pierre Barou.[1] They claimed that it insulted Gorbachev. I was against any retraction, especially since the harshest words in that conversation were mine, not Andrei's. But the presence of several journalists constrained me, and Andrei gave in to their arguments. Yet just a few days ago one of them told me that now he thought that they had made a mistake in nagging Andrei into writing a statement of renunciation.

---

1. Parts of this interview appeared in *The New York Review*, March 2, 1989.

Another argument occurred when Boris Yeltsin asked Andrei to withdraw his candidacy in the Moscow National-Territorial District in exchange for Yeltsin's withdrawing as a candidate in another district, and Andrei agreed. In so-called real politics such agreements are acceptable; but the politics that was part of Sakharov's life had to be, and in fact was on an incomparably higher plane. There are enough "real" politicians without Sakharov. And so I considered this gentleman's agreement a mistake. It was done on the advice of several good people from the Memorial Society, who took an active part in Andrei's election campaign. In the second volume of his autobiography, *Moscow and Beyond*, Andrei Dmitrievich recalls these episodes.[2] Instead of describing the "mystery story of the book," however, I have been writing about our family life, which like everyone else's is always a series of arguments and reconciliations, but we had no other serious disagreements than these.

—*translated by Antonina Bouis*
October 10, 1991

---

2. Knopf, 1991.

18

ELIZABETH HARDWICK
ON MURRAY KEMPTON

FOR SOME YEARS Murray Kempton lived, as I do, on West 67th Street in Manhattan and so he was not only a friend but a neighbor. Every day of his adult life Murray wrote, since he was a practicing journalist with nightly deadlines to be met. When he was not at his desk, he was sure to be *talking* in a rather stately but never dominating manner. I sometimes met him when he was going off to work in the morning. There at the curb I never heard him speak of the weather even though in New York there is likely to be too much or too little of whatever mean is thought desirable. Instead, without preface, he would begin: "I don't know what to make of Philip Larkin's unpleasant letters. All that stuff about wogs and blacks is just a pose, because clever people like to pretend to be worse than they are." Or if he had his earphones on he might say: Perhaps there *is* something Nazi about Elisabeth Schwarzkopf's singing, but anyway God bless her.

Part of Murray's refinement was to be generous to the thieving and polite to the perfidious. In his loquacious individuality there was an absence of vehemence, all the more striking in a moralist, which he was, as well as being more or less a man of the left. In lacking the instinct or habit of vehemence of opinion he was free of the woeful predictability of ideologues of both the left and the right. The grudge, the storehouse of rancor, was not his style and perhaps in that way he was a little out-of-date in the present hyperbolic atmosphere. There he was in his Brooks Brothers suit, shirt, and tie, toting his pipe and briefcase, costumed for, perhaps, some minor but consoling corporate position. But solvency was hardly his fate since he was one who always managed to take on more obligation than income.

His prose style—there's that, noticeable as his very curly hair. Of course, Murray lived among and worked with colleagues who also had a style, which in the zoo of the arts is a sort of protective coloring like the stripes of a zebra. A demotic, urban, rapid mode is a gift but also an accomplishment, personal and defining, street-smart and artful—Jimmy Breslin comes to mind. Murray also went down to the courthouse, knew the pols, and gave thought to the felons, although what he wrote about those encountered there perhaps they could not always parse. In his columns, his style was closer to the nineteenth-century English historians and essayists than to the moderate cadence of, for instance, Walter Lippmann. I once or twice talked with him about the possible influence on his manner of the great Macauley. His reply would go something like this: I would not deign to hang my ragged pantaloons on the swallowtail coat of a lord.

After much procrastination, or perhaps modest reluctance for whatever reason, he brought to publication a selection of his work to accompany a previous one that appeared in 1963. He gave it the title *Rebellions, Perversities, and Main Events.* It is a beautiful book with some almost forgotten public figures brought back to mind, along with mischievous undertakings by those still more or less fresh. Tribulations, misadventures, and occasional escapes from retribution are here *memorialized*, a word not altogether indolent since in other hands than Murray's the ill-thought-of would have fared much worse.

Westbrook Pegler: He never told a lie that he had not told himself first.

Roy Cohn: Was commencing to look like some priapic statue incautiously bought at the flea market and left out too long in the garden rains.

Gordon Liddy: At his worst, there was something comforting about Liddy; there will always be plots against human liberty, and how can we be safer than with someone this certain to mess up their execution? Not the least of his manifold talents is for getting caught.

Michael Milken: However we may despair of ever touching the infinite, we never so sense its presence as when we contemplate the sincerity of the swindler.

The disreputable brought to public notice were not always the object of Murray's reflections; he went to art galleries, read poetry and history, and traveled abroad. Still, when he goes to Italy, what you might call Murray-Kempton-events will appear unbidden with an impish mockery. He is in Sicily in the ancient Greek city of Syracuse on the Ionian Sea, lodging in the old part of town among ruins of temples and fountains, walking on the ground that had known the footsteps of Plato, Pindar, and Aeschylus. The ancient theater remains with its stone seats sloping down to the stage. A poster announces that there is to be in the hallowed amphitheater a jazz concert by Romano Mussolini, Romano being the youngest son of the misbegotten *duce* who passed down to his children a patrimony of one disaster after another. The poster leads Murray to imagine:

The Anglo-American fleet lowering upon the southern coast of Sicily, and in Rome, at the Villa Torlonia, Benito Mussolini upstairs abed under assault by his ulcers and intimations that it might all be coming apart, and downstairs little Romano listening to Count Basie on the American Armed Forces Radio and rejoicing that its signal was growing louder and louder.

Murray's funeral became him as his life did. It was held at Saint Ignatius of Antioch Episcopal Church, his church, and was to abide by his expressed wishes for the Burial Order in the Book of Common Prayer and that the *Sanctus*, *Benedictus* and the *Agnus Dei* by Byrd be sung. I was reminded of a wedding once held in my apartment and presided over by the classics scholar Moses Hadas of Columbia University. As he rose to begin, he glanced at the secular group assembled and said: "I suppose there's to be no mention of the Deity."

At Murray's funeral there was much mention of the Deity, but he had asked that his own name not be mentioned, and thereby precluded the testimony of friends, offerings so likely to be, in my experience, somewhat jocular in order to soothe the bereaved with memories of happier days. At the end of the service a bell was struck for each of the seventy-nine years of the deceased. It was a sound of incredible beauty as each tolling soulfully drifted off until the next year was struck. We were on West End Avenue in Manhattan, a broad and practical city thoroughfare, but with the unearthly resonance of the service in the air we might have been in medieval Florence, in Italy, following the funeral cortege, black carriage, black horses along the cobbled street.

—June 12, 1997

19

AILEEN KELLY
ON ISAIAH BERLIN

FEW TEACHERS WILL ever be as much loved and mourned as Isaiah. As a graduate student at Wolfson College, Oxford, whose first president he became in the late 1960s, I was constantly made aware of my great luck: my choice of college within the University had brought me into the daily orbit of what we all sensed was the most fascinating, the most remarkable person we would ever encounter. Soon after I joined the College, he sent me a note asking me to come and discuss my research on the Russian intelligentsia. Out of nervousness I delayed replying until one day he descended on me at lunch, commanding me to come back with him to his office. I emerged nearly three hours later after a dazzling tour of the landscape of Russian thought combined with a passionate vindication of the subject of my research, which others had frequently urged me to change. In the Sixties Western liberal academics tended to regard the Russian intelligentsia mainly as fanatical precursors of communism. With a warmth that recreated them as persons, Isaiah defended them as worthy of admiration for their moral commitment to dispelling illusions about the world and our place in it.

Much of that afternoon we spent discussing Alexander Herzen, whom Isaiah described as his hero. Later that day I sought out his

essays on Herzen and came upon a precise description of my own
recent impressions:

> I was puzzled and overwhelmed, when I first came to know
> [him]—by this extraordinary mind which darted from one
> topic to another with unbelievable swiftness, with inexhaust-
> ible wit and brilliance; which could see in the turn of some-
> body's talk, in some simple incident, in some abstract idea, that
> vivid feature which gives expression and life. He had...a kind
> of prodigal opulence of intellect which astonished his audi-
> ence....[His talk] demanded of those who were with him not
> only intense concentration, but also perpetual alertness, be-
> cause you had always to be prepared to respond instantly. On
> the other hand, nothing cheap or tawdry could stand even half
> an hour of contact with him. All pretentiousness, all pompous-
> ness, all pedantic self-importance, simply fled from him or
> melted like wax before a fire.

Isaiah was citing a contemporary's portrait of Herzen. His own resemblance to that extraordinary figure was striking (many of us would
echo, with regard to Isaiah, Tolstoy's comment on Herzen—that he
had never met anyone with "so rare a combination of scintillating
brilliance and depth"), but his sense of affinity with Herzen was
based above all on a shared moral outlook. They both combined a
deep respect for honesty and purity of motivation with an unerring
ability to detect artificiality and self-deception in intellectual en-
deavor and everyday behavior. Students sensed that with Isaiah they
were not required to perform, amuse, or entertain, but simply to give
their best, and this paradoxically put us at ease with him, the more
so as we soon found out that straining to impress him was counter-
productive. (Once, hoping to be congratulated on the originality of

an essay I had given him for comment, I was chagrined to find that he had read the footnotes just as closely as the text and had unearthed some errors of fact which I had overlooked in my haste to impress.)

Isaiah's personality and utterances were the subject of continual discussion by the students of his College. His Russian connections and his exotic past provided much food for inventive speculation: Had the unusual circular hole in his ancient felt hat been acquired during hostile action somewhere in the Baltic states? More than once he walked unexpectedly into a room where a passable imitation of his own unforgettable voice was in full flow.

I believe that his true voice can be found at its clearest in his essays on Herzen. More self-revealing than anything else he ever wrote, they shed light on the most enduring mystery about him: his combination of what many have seen as a tragic vision of the world with an inexhaustible curiosity and an irrepressible sense of fun.

Isaiah can be said to have rediscovered Herzen, who he believed had either been ignored or misrepresented for so long because he had revealed a truth too bleak for most people to bear: that faith in universally valid formulas and goals was an attempt to escape from the unpredictability of life into the false security of fantasy. His devotion to Herzen remained undiminished to the end of his life. Not long ago he wrote reproaching me for obscuring the uniqueness of Herzen's contribution by drawing parallels between him and thinkers such as Mikhail Bakhtin who had considered similar problems: "I can think of none, but perhaps I am too fanatical an admirer." He often cited Herzen's phrase "history has no libretto": all questions make sense and must be resolved not in terms of final goals but of the specific needs of actual persons at specific times and places. Herzen, he wrote, believed "that the day and the hour were ends in themselves, not a means to another day or another experience."

Here we have the key to one of the central paradoxes of Isaiah. Although his diary was always full and he was scrupulous about keeping appointments, he never gave the impression of being in a hurry, of being distracted from a person or an issue by anticipation of the next person or problem in line. Young academics were often astonished (as I was in my first encounter with him) that so important and busy a man was prepared to give them so much of his time. An American Slavist whom I met recently at a conference recalled having sent him her first book, not expecting a reply. His warm and detailed response, she told me, had her walking on air for weeks. On the evening after his death I remembered him with a Russian colleague whom he had encouraged in the same way in Oxford many years ago. A *"svetlaia lichnost"* (luminous personality), she said.

But we would diminish him if we did not appreciate that the instinctive goodness we loved was coupled with a carefully thought-through moral vision of whose validity he earnestly sought to persuade us. One of its distinctive characteristics, which he saw embodied in Herzen, was the total absence of a utilitarian approach to people and events, an "unquenchable delight in the variety of life and the comedy of human character." This was also one of Isaiah's most entrancing qualities. I remember him as the only one of us to emerge unexasperated from an interminable and contentious College meeting, happily quoting Kant's statement that "from the crooked timber of humanity no straight thing can ever be made." He was convinced (again I quote him on Herzen) that there was value in the very irregularity of the structure of human beings, "which is violated by attempts to force it into patterns or straitjackets."

Like Herzen (and Schiller) he believed profoundly in the seriousness of the play of life and human creativity, and was easily drawn into all kinds of frivolity. One night after dinner at Wolfson he joined a conversation in which a student was explaining the board game

Diplomacy, where each player represented one of the Great Powers of pre-1914 Europe. He invited us to his house the following Sunday morning to initiate him into the game; he then gave an impressive performance as the Ottoman Empire.

I have another memory of him sitting on a bale of hay in his three-piece suit, complete with watch chain and hat, holding forth to a group of fascinated students at a bonfire party held in a damp field on the bank of the Isis, where the building of the new College was to start the next day. It was late evening; a more typical college president, having put in the obligatory early appearance, would have been long gone.

All those who knew him well were asked over the years to persuade him to write more and not to squander his gifts in conversation. Yet his profligacy has not prevented him from being recognized as one of the major liberal thinkers of the twentieth century, and he belongs to an even more select group who achieved harmony between their moral vision and their life. He showed us virtue in action, not as obedience to a set of rules but as a generous responsiveness to the creative possibilities of the present moment. One always came away from a few hours in his company with a sense of living more intensely, with all one's perceptions heightened, although the topics of conversation were often far from exalted. He much enjoyed exchanging news about the latest academic scandals in Oxford and Cambridge, and expected the exchange to be on equal terms: his view of humanity required that Cambridge should be as fertile a source of stories about human frailty as Oxford, and he was never disappointed. We had an unfinished debate lasting several years over the precise difference between a cad and a bounder; he could always find fresh examples of each to offer from among our mutual acquaintances.

He loved to gossip about the concerns and quarrels of nineteenth-century Russian thinkers as though they were our common friends, but there was a serious side to this entertainment. He had the greatest respect for these thinkers' commitment to acting out their beliefs in their daily lives, and fiercely championed them against what he perceived as misjudgments of their motives; our one painful difference was over the question of how Turgenev would have behaved under particular pressures.

Isaiah saw no contradiction between recognizing that moral ideals were not absolute and believing one's own ideals binding on oneself. Again, his model was Herzen, who, he tells us, for all his skepticism, had an unshakable belief in the sanctity of personal liberty and the noble instincts of the human soul, as well as a hatred of "conformism, cowardice, submission to the tyranny of brute force or pressure of opinion, arbitrary violence, and anxious submissiveness... the worship of power, blind reverence for the past, for institutions, for mysteries or myths; the humiliation of the weak by the strong, sectarianism, philistinism, the resentment and envy of majorities, the brutal arrogance of minorities." Here, albeit in the third person, is Isaiah's profession of faith, in his own cadences.

He admired Herzen more than Turgenev because while neither had any illusions about the permanence of human existence and human values, Turgenev had achieved a cool detachment from the struggles and triumphs of contingent life, while Herzen "cared far too violently"; his realism was therefore the more courageous. In his last years Isaiah confronted the tragic side of his own philosophy with the same unflinching directness as his hero. On arriving for dinner in Cambridge sixteen months ago, he told me that something "very terrible" concerning him had just appeared in the press. He would say no more about it and I assumed it was some adverse review. The next day I found the interview, reprinted in the London *Times*, in which he reflects on his own death, declaring that, much though he would like it to be otherwise, the idea that there was some world in which there would be perfect truth, love, justice, and happiness made no sense in any conceptual scheme he knew. It was just a comforting idea for people who could not face the possibility of total extinction. But, he adds, "I wouldn't mind living on and on.... I am filled with curiosity and long to know, what next?

—December 18, 1997

20

MURRAY KEMPTON
ON FRANK SINATRA

FRANK SINATRA EVER did the fullest duty to his art, and now he is leaving us with the duty to sum him up. My betters have already done that. One day I was dealing with Ella Fitzgerald, and the subject of Sinatra came up and her intruder-mistrusting voice suddenly softened and she said, "Frank. Just this little guy telling this story. That's all you have to be."

In 1956, Nelson Riddle thought to employ the Hollywood String Quartet as backup for Sinatra's "Close to You" album. The HSQ found Sinatra as demanding as Schoenberg had been six years before, when it recorded "Verklärte Nacht" and so gratified its composer that he felt himself fully defined and registered his satisfaction by writing the liner notes. Sinatra asked not a whit less than Schoenberg, and Eleanor Aller, the HSQ's cellist, has remembered the delight of the challenge and fulfillment as "the sort of thing in which you just enjoy every minute, because the man is so musical."

And so those made newly aware of the summit of America-bred chamber music that was the Hollywood String Quartet would do well to catch those four on "The Lady Is a Tramp" and understand that the HSQ's glorious decade belongs not only to Schoenberg and Schubert but to Frank Sinatra, too.

For Frank Sinatra knew, as every artist must, that there is no such thing as trash that cannot be transcended. He also knew the second great lesson, which is that everything is there to be stolen if you have the taste to confine your larcenies to the worth-taking. We cannot appreciate the work if we overlook its elements of creative plagiarism.

The porkpie hat and the walk into the shadows of loneliness with the light at his back are all taken intact from the "One for My Baby" that Fred Astaire consummated in the unjustly forgotten movie *The Sky's the Limit*. I remember when Sinatra was trying to put together a sextet for the Kennedy Inaugural and finally had to tell Milton Berle, "Look, Milton, the only way you'll ever learn to sing is to listen to Billie Holiday and find out how to play out a note." The Lord had given him his voice; mother wit and a magpie's cunning account for the enduring distinction of the rest.

Our relations were always cordial, however fleeting, but it didn't take too long to recognize the puritanical little boy beneath the skin. Once we passed a few minutes after a Kennedy rally in Los Angeles. Sinatra was in the full fit of enchainment in the great clan's thrall, and said how great they all were: "Jack, Jackie, the ambassador, Bobby, and every one of them."

He had to confess, all the same, that he was coming to doubt that Peter Lawford, the brother-in-law, had the moral fiber befitting his grand connections.

"Do you mean to say," I, puzzled, asked, "that, when you and Sammy Davis throw a wild night, Peter Lawford comes along?"

"Yes," Sinatra replied. "That's just what I mean."

And he did, because at bottom he believed—and could rise every morning and believe again—that love is eternal and fidelity is a sacred trust. There and only there was his secret. What would *Don Giovanni* be except merely coarse *bouffe* if the Don could not so unvaryingly persuade himself that each fresh object of trifling fancy is his lifetime's love?

No, if you want to know why Frank Sinatra will intrude himself into the bloodstream of our memories if we survive to a hundred and five, forget the grown man he never became and look for the little boy he could not quite stop being, because that is the little boy who goes about searching for and singing about the love that will always last.

—June 25 1998

21

ADAM MICHNIK
ON ZBIGNIEW HERBERT

HE MARKED HIS epoch. He was a powerful essayist, an author of remarkable plays, and a poet of genius. He created his own language, a language of humble heroism, of self-ironic courage, and of romanticism—the romanticism of a soul that cherishes the classical canon of beauty, the European way of being Polish.

As a poet, he kept telling, with a proud determination, of a conquered and humbled Poland, of her sad dignity in a time when only her dreams had not been humiliated. In his life, he wrote the most magnificent pages in the book of Polish honor.

His language was of transparent beauty, conscious of its own fragility. Yet he was able to link these tender and fragile words in such a way that they became as hard as metal. "Be faithful Go": this sentence will reverberate in the Polish language forever.

He was formed by an epoch of spiritual confrontation with totalitarian barbarism, which he resisted with exemplary consistency. In the Seventies and Eighties, the poems of Zbigniew Herbert became a prayer of my generation; Mister Cogito became our guide through difficult times in which a monster ruled.

That monster:

is difficult to describe
escapes definition

it is like an immense depression
spread out over the country

it can't be pierced
with a pen
with an argument
or spear

were it not for its suffocating weight
and the death it sends down
one would think
it is the hallucination
of a sick imagination

but it exists
for certain it exists

like carbon monoxide it fills
houses temples markets

poisons wells
destroys the structures of the mind
covers bread with mold

the proof of the existence of the monster
is its victims

it is not direct proof
but sufficient[1]

The poet struggled against this monster without pause. In that fight, he could be subtle, but he also could be brutal—striking too hard, or blindly. Always, however, he reached back for the "power of taste," which forced the poet to rise to the occasion—to look fate squarely in the face.

Now he has been received into the circle of cold skulls—the circle of Gilgamesh, Hector, Roland, defenders of the borderless kingdom and of the city of ashes, into the circle of Kochanowski, Mickiewicz, Slowacki.

Zbigniew Herbert is today mourned by all Poland, by people of all ideological stripes and literary sympathies. When he was pronouncing on social and political matters, he did not depart from the norms of the Polish inferno that has engulfed us in recent years; but when he spoke in verse, he attained the perfection and wisdom of heart that belong only to masterpieces.

There were times when I had the privilege of being close to Zbigniew Herbert. His poems helped me survive the difficult years of prison. This I have never forgotten. Then our ways violently parted. In recent years I was often unable to understand his political statements. But his poems always brought me to enchantment and meditation.

And this is how it will remain:

The ditch where a muddy river flows
I call the Vistula. It is hard to confess:

---

1. Fragment of "The Monster of Mr. Cogito," from Zbigniew Herbert, *Report from the Besieged City and Other Poems*, translated by John and Bogdana Carpenter (Ecco Press, 1985).

they have sentenced us to such love
they have pierced us through with such a fatherland[2]

—*Translated from the Polish by Irena Grudzinska Gross*
October 22, 1998

---

2 Fragment of "Prologue," translated by John and Bogdana Carpenter, from Zbigniew
Herbert, *Selected Poems* (Oxford University Press, 1977).

22

JOHN UPDIKE
ON SAUL STEINBERG

THE *NEW YORK TIMES* obituary quoted a fellow cartoonist as saying, "Steinberg was not a warm man. He was chilly and Olympian with a somewhat hauteur tone [*sic*]," but in my slight acquaintance with him he consistently appeared gracious and kind. Our acquaintance was slight but long: in 1945 I wrote him from my small town in Pennsylvania asking that he send me, for no reason except that I wanted it, the original of a drawing I had seen in *The New Yorker*, of one man tipping his hat and another tipping back his hat with his head still in it. At this time I was an avariciously hopeful would-be cartoonist of twelve or thirteen and Steinberg a thirty-one-year-old Romanian Jew whose long American sojourn had begun but four years before. Perhaps he thought that his new citizenship entailed responding to importunities from unknown American adolescents. He sent me not the original but a duplicate he had considerately made, with his unhesitant pen, and inscribed it, in impeccable New World fashion, "To John Updike with best wishes." Nearly fifty years later, when I turned sixty, he sent me a pencil drawing of a rabbit on a fragmentary table drawing a Steinbergian scroll, with the inscription "John Up 60! Love from Saul ST."

He would not, perhaps, like having these small personal generosities broadcast in this telling; his sensibility was fertile but fastidious, expressed in the haute-bourgeois polish of his tailoring and the soft but distinct phrasing of his speech, as if he were translating, with a barely perceptible hesitation, out of an arcane, possibly wordless inner language. He spoke not exactly with an accent but with an un-American tendency toward epigrammatic precision. He made little of his Romanian origins; "pure Dada," he called his native land. Yet if one thinks of the Romanians, all exiles, that have figured prominently in the culture of the twentieth century—Brancusi, Ionesco, Tristan Tzara, the aphorist E. M. Cioran—one glimpses a shared economy, a willingness to invent visionary forms and to seek a comprehensive simplicity. Ambitions so innocently sweeping might have less easily arisen among natives of a less marginal European country, with enough gravity of tradition to hold creative spirits in place.

* * *

Steinberg studied and made his artistic beginnings in that lightest-hearted of major nations, Italy, receiving in 1940 a doctoral degree in an architecture he never practiced but whose linear basis and laden notation infused his innovations in cartooning. His father was a printer and bookbinder who became a manufacturer of cardboard boxes, preparing the way for his son's mature romance with paper, with alphabets, with trademarks and documents and maps and fingerprints and rubber stamps and all such variegated fauna of the two-dimensional, man-created world. Hilton Kramer, one of the many art critics provoked to wit by Steinberg's own, wrote, "There is a kind of primitivism in all this, an animism, for everything in Steinberg—even the most inanimate object or abstract thought—is teeming with aspiration, ambition and portents." The power to generate images was never merely a means to an end for Steinberg; imagery was, itself, a matter for celebration. Those deadpan postcard-shaped images he produced in the Seventies of middling American post offices and banks and motels and Main Streets carried his joy in the joke of image to a delicate extreme—like those sometimes three-dimensional table tops and desk tops he rendered in the same period, rectilinear homage to what simply is, things here and there and the ominous blankness of the table or the prairie pressing through in the spaces between.

Like Nabokov and Milos Forman, to name just two other affectionate adult immigrants, Steinberg saw America afresh, with details to which natives had grown blind or numb. American parades, American cowboys, American mountains of Art Deco, New York taxis in their screaming, bulbous decor, the quaint gingerbread pomp of suburban mansions and railroad stations—these visual events were mixed, not so paradoxically, with the emblems of the intended Utopia, the Latinate slogans involving Lex and Lux and Pax and Tax and Vox Populi, the Statue of Liberty enjoying her deadpan marriage with Uncle Sam, the practical partnership of S. Freud and S. Claus.

When, from the window of his studio on Union Square, Steinberg saw the great American city descending into a Walpurgisnacht of whoredom and homelessness and what he called "Mickey Mouse brutality," he sought for the visual vocabulary to render it and came up with roachlike pedestrians scrabbling along amid giant congealed automobiles, and implacable Amazons whose high-heeled boots ended at their necks, and tall Mickey Mouses blandly toting machine guns. Steinberg's fine doodling pen line—a handwriting of the mind, a punning seismograph—turned to relatively coarse and indefinite pencil and crayon, deployed in clashing, scrawled mimesis of a perceived ugliness; his art became ever more a gallery art, aimed at collectors and couched in a private symbology. *The New Yorker* of this time, liberally race-blind to the point that blacks had not appeared in its cartoons for decades, could not have found it easy to accommodate a vision so macabre and grim, so culturally diverse and unwinsomely grotesque, but in fact it did salvage a few covers from Steinberg's Boschian visions.

He and William Shawn shared some points of sensibility—laconic, quietly erudite men with a taste for the quizzically existential. If the *pièce de résistance* of an issue of Harold Ross's magazine was a lusty Arno cartoon, that of one of Shawn's was a Steinberg spread, often some delicious example of synesthesia such as the sounds of different musical instruments seen as clouds and swirls of abstraction or a page of "Country Noises" heard as typographical borders and ornaments. A reader could study it lovingly, as the joke unfolded its several levels. Steinberg came to English late (while waiting to be admitted to this country in Santo Domingo, he read *Huckleberry Finn* for practice) and its basic vocabulary kept a primal kinesis for him: one *New Yorker* cover shows "Today" blasting off from a crumbling "Yesterday" on a route plotted "Breakfast Lunch Dinner Tomorrow." On another, "I HAVE" hangs like dirty wash on the terra firma of "I AM" while the O in "I DO" shines above like the sun. On others, an army of "WE ARE"s being led by "I SHALL" carries the banner "ARE WE?"; the M and W of "HOW" and "MYTH" are the mouths of fish about to eat up "WHY?" and "TRUTH"; and the letter E wistfully dreams of "É."

Within the magazine, until Steinberg's ambitions overflowed the spot cartoon, one encountered people with zigzag faces who seemed to be both coming and going, and a man shooting an apple off his own head, and a woman with a vase for a head, with the flower of a thought in it. A businessman talks a torrent of scribbled words inside a speech balloon shaped grandly "NO." Speech balloons, those indispensable aerial platters in comic strips, show up sideways in the mouths of alligators, and tucked under people's arms like baguettes, and mimicking a street map of Paris or (a competing vacation in a luncheon chat) the island of Sardinia. And so abundantly on. Such an inventory dulls, perhaps, the surprise with which one encountered a Steinberg, in pages where—the half-blind scrawls of Thurber aside—the cartoons, whether by Arno or Whitney Darrow or Garrett Price, showed a solid representational technique. One did not open *The New Yorker* then prepared to find a nude photograph or a headline-making exposé; a spiky Steinberg fancy was as exciting an ornament as one might encounter on those good gray lawns of well-weeded prose.

As the Abstract Expressionists forced us to know that we were looking at paint, Steinberg compelled us to realize we were looking at ink. His drawings turned a corner in mental space and left the looker disoriented; in his ceaseless effort to explore the spaces of transformation, Steinberg resorted to three dimensions, painting imaginary women seated on the edge of real bathtubs, and men sedately folding themselves into cardboard boxes. He worked in wood, creating unopenable books with inviting titles—equivalents of his elegantly penned documents that cannot be read. He drew on photographs of junk-store furniture, of crumpled paper, and of New York rooftops. He drew awninged front entrances on sheets of graph paper, turning them into skyscrapers. To call these inventions "visual puns" is to make them sound slighter than they are; they are wormholes between different universes that are simultaneously contiguous and parsecs apart. He created for himself a unique niche between high art and commercial cartooning—a niche in which he, perhaps, was not always comfortable. The *Times* quoted him as saying, "The art world doesn't quite know where to place me."

But in his restlessness he resisted being placed. The huge and legal-headache-making celebrity of his image of the world as seen looking west from Ninth Avenue—the typical New Yorker's dismissively foreshortened perspective, *The New Yorker*'s cover for March 29,

1976—may mark a moment after which his work became less ingratiating and more restless. A great deal of his later *oeuvre* is scattered in gallery catalogs. One would be happy, now, for a retrospective album that would reach back, if possible, to the cartoons he published as a student in Milan, and the propaganda drawings he did for the OSS as an American soldier, to be dropped behind enemy lines to encourage anti-German resistance. Something subversive remained in his art, undermining the intuitive connection between what we see and what we know, calling into question, like a good metaphysician, the bases of our experience. He was a comedian of epistemology, whose problematics engaged him; Descartes's formula "Cogito, ergo sum" more than once recurred among his verbal reifications. His cartoons, even the apparently simplest Möbius strip of a doodle, occur in a realm of thought where style is substance and double takes are the least we owe the artist. "Drawing is a way of reasoning on paper," he said. Steinberg never, even in his most extended illegible flourish, seemed other than reasonable, nor did we ever doubt that his was, somehow, a representation of the world we live in.

—June 24, 1999

23

JONATHAN MIRSKY
ON NOEL ANNAN

NOEL ANNAN, WHO contributed more than one hundred articles to these pages, was a wonderfully gifted and energetic writer, scholar, and administrator who claimed that any able person should be able to manage two full-time jobs simultaneously. He often did more. Noel was one of the few figures in English public life known simply by his first name. There was no mistaking him for anyone else.

In what to me is his most instructive, and funniest, book, *Changing Enemies: The Defeat and Regeneration of Germany* (1996), an account of his life during his twenties when he was very near the top of Allied intelligence during World War II, he recalled—as applicable to himself—Tyndall's translation of the Bible: "The Lorde was with Joseph, and he was a luckie feloe."

Choosing Tyndall's translation says something about Noel's sensitivity to language. His modesty, however, while charming, was unwarranted. At twenty-six he was a lieutenant-colonel in the British army handling some of the darkest secrets of the war. He was asked to help decide such questions as whether Hitler would invade Russia and whether Allied bombing was slowing the German war machine. Still very young, his German fluent, he had much to do with choosing Adenauer rather than the Socialist leader Kurt Schumacher as the man to lead Germany out of fascism and toward democracy. He admired Schumacher: "He was the sort of man whom intellectuals understand: very pure, very fierce, unwilling to compromise with the truth as he saw it.... I felt affection for him because I saw that he was doomed to defeat.... In my mind's eye I see myself smiling and grasping Schumacher's hand...while to Adenauer I bowed in respect and admiration."

All his life Noel understood that justice and right existed uneasily together. He wrote that justice stands "in the jar of the door which separates right and wrong." It was useless to subject the Germans to "continual acts of self-humiliation....The Western powers had to trust the German people to display some political sense." He saw Adenauer not only as the right man for the ultimate German job, but also as "cunning, sometimes ruthless, always an authoritarian... conscious of his goals and above all a man of limitless patience...an old man *not* in a hurry."

As for Churchill, he wrote, he was "a fascinator: but few have been more inconsiderate to those who served him or more ungrateful to friends who stood by him when he was in exile." And yet, for those who were young and worked under him, Noel concluded, Churchill was one of those men who "remain heroic figures, and their defects pale because they were then, and still appear, larger than life, men who enjoyed, as well as responded to, their call to destiny."

The last part of that description could be applied to Noel himself. Provost of King's College, Cambridge, when he was thirty-nine, he went on to head University College, London, become the first full-time vice-chancellor of the University of London, chairman of the trustees of the National Gallery, trustee of the British Museum, and a member of the board of the Royal Opera House. His Annan Report of 1977, proposing reforms in public broadcasting, would alone have been enough of an accomplishment for many men.

Yet he also wrote book after book and essay after essay, among them a biography of Leslie Stephen, still the necessary introduction to all studies of Bloomsbury; *Our Age: Portrait of a Generation*, a vast and entertaining survey of the intellectual aristocracy of Noel's generation; and, last year, *The Dons*, an account of the men who shaped Cambridge and Oxford. Noel's emotional and intellectual heart remained in Cambridge, where, largely from E. M. Forster, also a King's man, he absorbed the idea of friendship as having its own unmatched value. It was at Cambridge, too, that he learned about academic venom. F. R. Leavis, Noel observed, "cultivated to perfection the sneer, which he used like an oyster-knife, inserting it into the shell of his victim, exposing him with a quick turn of the wrist, and finally flipping him over and inviting his audience to disparage him as tainted and inedible." His own writing was exceptional not only for its wisdom and perception but for its lack of malice.

There is a photograph in *Changing Enemies* of the young Noel in 1943—elegant, slim, magnetic—gesturing to the Joint Intelligence Staff with both hands spread wide at a map. He was twenty-seven. I remember him that way in 1954, lecturing on political theory to undergraduates at Cambridge; we dropped our usual blasé indifference because he thrilled us. It was the same within King's when I met him for "supervisions," or tutorials, each week. Most of our supervisors seemed to be going through the motions, assigning the same essays each week, year after year, tending to doze as we read them aloud. To be taught by Noel was an entirely different experience. At the end of each session he would ask eagerly, "Now, what do you want to write for next week?" While the new essay was being read, Noel would say, "Ah, yes, exactly," or "I hadn't thought of that," or he would ask a challenging question. When I told him that late-eighteenth- and early-nineteenth-century French history bored me, he pressed into my hands *The Red and the Black*. "Read that, my dear fellow; don't bother to write an essay for next week. Just tell me if you're still bored."

Three years ago, when he was almost eighty, Noel wrote to me, "I regard the future with gloom." The rest of the closely typed two pages was crammed with a detailed analysis of the men who had taught me, a flash or two into the intrigues of the intelligence world, and an invitation to lunch at "the palace of Westminster [the House of Lords] which I attend." Noel delighted in observing intellectual life and politics and in tracing the vagaries of class in each, as he showed in the many remarkable essays he wrote for this journal. He could have been writing about himself—maybe he was—when he remembered, of the great men he knew in his youth, their "peculiar blend of gaiety, enjoyment of life, contempt for dull, grey, prudent policy, that spontaneity and imaginative belief in a better or a more glorious world, [which] is something that has disappeared from public life at the end of this century."

—April 13, 2000

24

ALISON LURIE
ON EDWARD GOREY

EDWARD GOREY, WHO died on April 15, was associated with *The New York Review of Books* from the beginning. His fantastic and memorable cover illustrations were a feature of every anniversary issue; and in 1975 he contributed an ongoing serial, *Les Mystères de Constantinople*, whose heroine was thought by some to resemble one of the *NYR*'s editors.

To enter the world of Edward Gorey is to step into a kind of parallel Gothic universe, full of haunted mansions, strange topiary, and equally haunted and strange human beings. Though they are mainly well meaning and well dressed and live in surroundings of slightly decaying Victorian or Edwardian luxury, they tend to seem baffled or oppressed by life. They play croquet and go on picnics and have elaborate tea parties, but somehow something always goes wrong. There are sudden deaths and disappearances, and they are often haunted, not only by ghosts but by strange creatures of all sorts, some of which resemble giant bugs, while others suggest hairy wombats or small winged lizards.

In many of these books, children especially are at risk: they fall victim to natural disasters, are carried off by giant birds, or eaten by comic monsters like the Wuggly Ump. In *The Gashlycrumb Tinies* every letter of the alphabet announces the death of a little girl or boy. Yet somehow the overall effect is not tragic, but comic—just as it is in the work of Edward Lear, whom Gorey greatly admired.

In these macabre comedies, almost no one looks happy—with the striking exception of the cats, who always seem to be having a wonderful time, especially on the covers of two of the anthologies of Gorey's work, *Amphigorey* and *Amphigorey Too*. As might be suspected, Gorey was remarkably fond of cats. According to report, he never had fewer than five at any one time, and whenever I visited his apartment in Manhattan I had the distinct impression that there were at least seven or eight, all of them looking extremely contented and well fed, even smug.

Among Edward Gorey's other enthusiasms were Victorian novels, silent films, and the New York City Ballet, all of which provided inspiration for his work. His passion for the productions of George Balanchine and the principal dancers Diana Adams and Patricia McBride was so great that for many years he attended every performance of a Balanchine work. After Balanchine's death he moved with his cats to Cape Cod, where he had a large extended family and many friends.

Though Edward Gorey always denied being inspired by real life, I have sometimes thought that one of his early works, *The Doubtful Guest*, which was dedicated to me, was partly a comment on my inexplicable (to him) decision to reproduce. The title character in this book is smaller than anyone in the family it appears among. It has a peculiar appearance at first and does not understand language. As time passes it becomes greedy and destructive: it tears pages out of books, has temper tantrums, and walks in its sleep. Yet nobody even tries to get rid of the creature; their attitude toward it remains one of resigned acceptance. Who is this Doubtful Guest? The last page of the story makes everything clear:

It came seventeen years ago—and to this day
It has shown no intention of going away.

Of course, after about seventeen years, most children leave home.

In Edward Gorey's books death is often met with indifference. Not so in real life. The website maintained by his fans (www.goreyography) has already recorded scores of messages of shock, grief, and passionate admiration from correspondents aged thirteen to eighty. Many describe their surprise and joy when they first saw Gorey's work, and declare that they have found friends and lovers through a mutual appreciation of his books; others declare that they have rejected those who disliked Gorey—a decision I can well understand.

The loss of Edward Gorey is not only the loss of a brilliant and original writer and illustrator, but of a gifted stage and costume designer. He has also taken with him many other greatly talented people, notably Ogdred Weary, author of *The Curious Sofa* and *The Beastly Baby*; and Mrs. Regera Dowdy, author of *The Pious Infant* and translator of Eduard Blutig's *The Evil Garden*. (Critics claim that all these writers, and several others, are pseudonyms—and in some cases, anagrams—of Edward Gorey; but if we accept this we must also accept the astounding fact that Mr. Gorey produced over a hundred books.)

Often, characters in Gorey's books who die or disappear leave only a void behind: empty cross-hatched streets and withered formal gardens and rooms with strange wallpaper. We are luckier.

—May 25, 2000

25

IAN BURUMA
ON JOHN SCHLESINGER

WHEN MY UNCLE John Schlesinger was preparing the script for his film *Sunday, Bloody Sunday* in 1970, he went for a walk with his father. My grandfather, by then a retired pediatrician, asked John what his new film was about. John explained that it was about a gay Jewish doctor (Peter Finch) who loved a young man (Murray Head) who also loved a woman (Glenda Jackson).

My grandfather thought this over carefully, and said: "But John, did you really have to make him Jewish as well?" This is the kind of family we come from: loving, tolerant, encouraging, and very keen to be British, without drawing unnecessary attention to our non-British roots. The Schlesingers did their best to fit in. A shared love of Wagner's operas (handed down by my great-grandfather, an Orthodox Jew; the other great-grandfather was a secular man; he liked Brahms) is just about all that remains of our German-Jewish background. My grandparents were British in the way their parents were German, that is, very, but without ever taking it for granted.

John never fitted in, and that is partly what made him an artist. His earliest ambition was to be a cinema organist. He was mesmerized, as a child, by those glamorous figures, bathed in light, who would slowly descend into the orchestra pit when the main entertainment began. To be entertaining was an imperative with John. My earliest memories of him are of his doing conjuring tricks for us, or imitating sinister German accents, or impersonating the Queen of Holland. One also felt, from a very early age, that to arrest his attention one had to amuse him in return, which was not always easy. This extended to his professional life. He was a superb director of actors—Julie Christie, Alan Bates, Dustin Hoffman, and the list goes on—but could be hard on them too.

No good at sports, John was deeply unhappy at his private boarding school, which, like most such institutions, saw sportsmanship as the highest masculine virtue. His father hoped that school would make a man of him. Perhaps in a way it did. John once told me that his homosexual inclinations were the one thing that put him in the mainstream of school life.

John ran away from school once or twice, and felt a failure. What kept him going was the prospect of the holidays, when he would cast his brothers, sisters, and cousins in elaborate plays, performed for the whole family. He took this very seriously. Rehearsal schedules and costume designs were meticulously prepared. The other bright spot in his schooldays, apart from music, which he loved, was the gift of a 9.5 mm movie camera from his grandmother. An early work—heard about, but never seen by me—shows the school's headmaster changing into his bathing costume.

John's first proper film, *The Black Legend*, shot in 16 mm while he was a student at Oxford, and financed by his doting grandmother, was also a family affair. Made near the family home in Berkshire in 1948, this eighteenth-century tale of a couple being hanged on Inkpen Beacon for adultery already shows remarkable technical skill, as well as John's taste for the macabre and hatred of intolerance. The famous movie critic Dilys Powell praised the film, which encouraged him to carry on. He was also an actor in student productions, and toured the US with the Oxford Players.

Like other Englishmen, John was called up for military service. But army life was not for him. He told the army board that he was "a Jew and proud of it," which may not have unsettled the officers particularly but rather outraged my grandfather. He then proceeded to mislay his gun. Still haunted by a sense of failure, he found more congenial company in ENSA, the army's entertainment division. He did conjuring tricks for the troops in Singapore.

Although a great mimic and raconteur, John was a competent rather than a fine actor. His roles varied from pantomime dames to villains in television episodes of *Ivanhoe*, played by Roger Moore, and he appeared as one of Robin Hood's Merry Men, directed by Lindsay Anderson. None of this was of great consequence, but he did get to see a superb director at work by appearing in Michael Powell's *Oh...Rosalinda!!* (1955). He also had a small part as a German POW in *The Battle of the River Plate* (1956), for which he rehearsed his one line in German with his grandmother from Kassel, who happened to be the aunt of Franz Rosenzweig, the religious philosopher.

It was as a documentary filmmaker for the BBC that John began to find his true métier. In 1961, his brilliant, witty record of a day at Waterloo Station, entitled *Terminus*, won prizes and led to his first feature film, *A Kind of Loving* (1962). Adapted from a novel by Stan Barstow, it was a typical example of kitchen sink drama, then much in fashion. Fed up with stories about plummy people lounging around London drawing rooms, young, often leftist, directors, such as Lindsay Anderson and Karel Reisz, turned to working-class life in the industrial north of England.

This may not have been quite John's scene; he was not particularly left-wing for a start. But his feeling of not fitting in, of being a failure, gave him a deep sympathy for losers, dreamers, and fantasists. Vic

(Alan Bates), a young man trapped in a marriage with Ingrid (June Ritchie), is such a man, fighting against and then resigning himself to the constraints of living with his bride and her ghastly mother. *A Kind of Loving* is the first film I saw John shoot. All I can remember is Thora Hird, as the mother-in-law, telling Vic: "You've got to make your sacrifices." Which, come to think of it, is rather typical for John's concern with life's limitations.

Billy, the main character in *Billy Liar* (1963), is a pure fantasist. A clerk at a provincial undertaker's, Billy (Tom Courtenay) imagines himself to be everything he is not: an upper-class toff, a conquering general, a great dictator, a war hero. When, at the end of the film, he has to choose between escaping to London with Julie Christie or continuing his life as a dreamer in a dreary north country town, he chooses the latter. It is a choice John himself might not have made, but he understood it.

Joe Buck (Jon Voight), the would-be hustler of rich and beautiful New York women in *Midnight Cowboy* (1969), is a much raunchier, American version of Billy; a down-and-out country boy who lives much of his life in his somewhat junky fantasies, culled from TV, advertising, and the movies. I was once told by John that Gore Vidal, when asked to write the script, did not believe anyone would be interested in "some dumb cowboy." But it was precisely the humanity of the born loser that interested John. What redeems this character is his love for another deadbeat, the limping Ratso (Dustin Hoffman). John used all his documentary skills to bring the underbelly of Manhattan, the world of (pre-Disney) 42nd Street hustlers and junkies, alive. He often said that a similar film could not be made in America today.

Much as John empathized in his films with street people, provincial dreamers, and other oddballs, his own life remained quite solidly anchored in his family. He had no children of his own but was attached to all of us. After my grandmother, a matriarch of the old school, died, he became, as it were, the patriarch who kept the family together. Annual celebrations revolved around him. His achievements allowed us to bask in vicarious glory. Movie stars would smile politely, as we were proudly presented as "my nephew" or "my niece." It was to John that most of us went, when in trouble. His attentiveness to our problems was actually quite remarkable, especially since one was always aware that part of his mind, like Billy Liar's or Joe Buck's, was usually drifting off somewhere far away.

Family man and misfit; it was this combination that enabled him to look at life from the outside, while remaining on the inside. Perhaps a Jewish background, no matter how assimilated, allowed for a similarly off-center perspective on British society, which he regarded with great affection and almost constant irritation. He loved the English landscape, celebrated in his underrated adaptation of Thomas Hardy's *Far from the Madding Crowd* (1967), and cherished many British institutions, including the royal family. He shared with others of his generation an odd veneration for the Queen Mother. But he loathed the narrow horizons of English life, the attitude of "Oh, no, we couldn't possibly do that. That's not the way we do things here."

What attracted him to America was precisely the opposite: its openness and enthusiasm. But John's Britishness colored his view of the US too, sometimes to great comic effect—Joe Buck's bus ride to New York in *Midnight Cowboy*—but a supercilious European disdain for America could sometimes make his satire go over the top, as in the great flop of his career, a screwball comedy about hucksterism in small-town Florida, entitled *Honky-Tonk Freeway* (1981).

Despite some notable American successes, I believe John's best films were set in England. There he could be satirical without disdain. Just as Robert Altman's acid views of America are tempered by love, John's attachment to his native country stayed his heavy-handed tendencies. This shows in some of his late films, such as *Cold Comfort Farm* (1995), and especially in *An Englishman Abroad* (1983) and *A Question of Attribution* (1992), the two short films about Guy Burgess and Anthony Blunt, written by Alan Bennett for the BBC. John's (and Bennett's) take on the two gay Englishmen who spied for the Soviet Union is compassionate without being sentimental about what they did. In a way, Burgess and Blunt fit perfectly in John's long line of misfits, very British even at the heart of the British establishment, and at the same time on the outside, dreaming of a fantasy world where they might be heroes: Billy Liars spying for Stalin.

John's success with Bennett's scripts showed how much he depended on good writers. He did not get on particularly well with Penelope Gilliatt, but his best film of all, in my opinion, is *Sunday, Bloody Sunday*, which she wrote in close cooperation with John. It is also his most personal work. There is a great deal of John in the doctor, who dutifully attends every family occasion, but might be found cruising for a pickup in Picadilly after the festivities are over.

What made this such a bold film, especially for its time, is the middle-class normality of the subjects' lives. Audiences were used to seeing flamboyant queens fluttering their wrists and saying "ducky" or "darling," or "she" when they meant "he," but here was a nice doctor, without a trace of camp, kissing a young man on the mouth before planning a joint holiday to Italy. The extraordinary scene where Peter Finch speaks directly to the camera, and talks about having to share his lover with another person, is typical of John's attitude to life. Whereas the woman in the triangle wishes to give up her lover, because she wants all or nothing, the doctor says half a loaf is still better than no loaf.

John made homosexual love look perfectly natural, and by doing so struck a bigger blow for emancipation than most demonstrations could ever achieve. If he had regrets at the end of his life, I think it was that he did not take this theme further. When he was recovering from a severe stroke, I asked him whether his illness had made him think differently of his life and work. Yes, he whispered, it had. It was about his films. He wished he had done more on "sexuality."

John was not by nature a joiner of political parties or movements. He was not especially interested in politics. In his life, as in his films, he was a humanist. His favorite directors—Satyajit Ray, de Sica, Truffaut—were rather like him, often funny, somewhat pessimistic, but always humane. Unlike Lindsay Anderson, or Kenneth Tynan, or other angry young men of the 1950s, John didn't see art as a tool of politics. Tolerance, not revolution is what he pleaded for. This did not make him especially popular with radical gay activists, or indeed with some of the more "engaged" artists of his generation. He was a misfit even there.

What interested him most was relationships, between men and women, or men and men, or parents and children, and how people cope with their limitations. This made him a brilliant observer. Nothing escaped his sharp eye for the quirkiest nuances of human behavior. On the top of his form, this made him one of the great directors of our time. In private, it made him more than an uncle; more an example, which we will never match, but always cherish.

—September 25, 2003

26

DARRYL PINCKNEY
ON ELIZABETH HARDWICK

IN THE FALL of 1973, she told her creative writing students at Barnard College, "There are really only two reasons to write: desperation or revenge." She used to tell us that we couldn't be writers if we couldn't be told no, if we couldn't take rejection. We supposed, therefore, that the tone she took with us was merely to get us ready: "I'd rather shoot myself than read that again." That writing could not be taught was clear from the way she shrugged her shoulder and lifted her beautiful eyes after this or that student effort. However, a passion for reading could be shared, week after week. "The only way to learn to write is to read." She brought in Boris Pasternak's *Safe Conduct*, translated by Beatrice Scott. She said she hated to do something so "pre-Gutenberg," and then began to read to us in a voice that was surprisingly high, loud, and suddenly very Southern:

> The beginning of April surprised Moscow in the white stupor of returning winter. On the seventh it began to thaw for the second time, and on the fourteenth when Mayakovsky shot himself, not everyone had yet become accustomed to the novelty of spring.

When she got to the line about the black velvet of the talent in himself, she stopped and threw herself back in her chair, curls trembling. Either we got it or we didn't, but it was clear from the way she struck her breastbone that to get it was, for her, the gift of life.

Sometimes she read in order to write, in order to begin, to find her way in. She agreed with Virginia Woolf that to read poetry before you wrote could open the mind. She typed at a desk upstairs in her apartment on West 67th Street; she typed at her heavy machine on the dining room table. She wrote in big handwriting on legal pads that then waited on end tables for her doubts; she wrote in little notebooks that she tucked between the cushions of the red velvet sofa. When she wrote, books piled up all around her, opened, or face down, each asking questions of her, whispering about the way in.

She remembered Hannah Arendt visiting Mary McCarthy in Maine. Arendt was lying on a sofa, with her arms behind her head, staring at the ceiling. "What's she doing?" she remembered asking. "She's *thinking*," her old friend Mary answered. She said she felt not a little put in her place. She said she envied those who could compose in their heads. She, however, did not know what she thought until she'd written it down. She said her first drafts always read as if they'd been written by a chicken. But when she revised, she did not question why she had chosen this life. She said that writing was almost a physical process and she could never understand why she could do it on, say, Tuesday, but not on Friday. She worked all the time, thinking about what she was doing, chin on hand, or, during the Golden Age of Smoking, cigarette poised between thumb and index finger, palm turned upward. She sat there until she found her way in, until she got it right, until it was finished.

She said what she liked most was cleaning up afterward, putting the books away, dispensing with the worksheets. Her chores distracted from the anxious wait until Robert Silvers called her and this great ally of her art never kept her waiting long. She said the problem with writing anything, poem, essay, or novel, was that once you were finished, you had to do it all over again, had to start on something new. Writing was not a collaboration. In the solitude of the blank page, everyone was up against the limits of himself or herself.

After Robert Lowell was gone, she said what she minded most was everyone forgetting how hard Harriet's father worked. He gave her the name Old Campaigner. To call her Old Campaigner, to remind her of the honor, never failed to bring forth that smile. Maybe he'd been thinking of the girl holding hands with her father and weeping in front of the radio down there in Kentucky the night Joe Louis lost. She said the faithful didn't know what hit them when she let them have it over the Moscow trials. Up from Trotsky in Lexington, out of John Donne in Morningside Heights, this white girl novelist of the misunderstood, lipstick terror of *Partisan Review*. Old Campaigner, the wife and understander who refused to go with him to visit Ezra Pound.

"All air and nerve, like nobody's business," her best friend Barbara Epstein used to say. She warned against perfectionism. She said it was self-sabotage; it only looked like genius. She cursed her perfectionism. Yet it cannot be imitated, the miraculous purity of her style, the soulfulness of her voice:

Oh, M, when I think of the people I have buried. And what of "the dreadful cry of murdered men in forests." Tell me, dear M, why it is that we cannot keep the note of irony, the tinkle of carelessness at a distance? Sentences in which I have tried for a certain light tone—many of those have to do with events, upheavals, destructions that caused me to weep like a child. Some removals I have not gotten over and I am, like everyone else, an amputee. (Why do I put in "like everyone else"? I fear that if I say that I am an amputee, and more so than anyone else, I will be embarrassing, over-reaching, yet in my heart I do believe I am more damaged than most.)

O you could not know
That such swift fleeing
No soul foreseeing—
Not even I—would undo me so!

I hate the glossary, the concordance of truth that some have about my real life—have like an extra pair of spectacles. I mean that such fact is to me a hindrance to composition. Otherwise I love to be known by those I care for and consequently am always on the phone, always writing letters, always waking up to address myself to B. and D. and E.—those whom I dare not ring up until the morning and yet must talk to throughout the night.

Now, my novel begins. No, now I begin my novel—and yet I cannot decide whether to call myself I or she.[1]

—February 14, 2008

---

1. From "Writing a Novel," published in *The New York Review*, October 18, 1973. The excerpt was the opening of a semi-autobiographical work that later became *Sleepless Nights*, which was first published in 1979 and has been reissued by New York Review Books.

27

COLIN THUBRON
ON PATRICK LEIGH FERMOR

WHEN PATRICK LEIGH Fermor died in June at the age of ninety-six, it seemed as if an era had come to an end. He was the last of a generation of warrior–travel writers that included the Arabian explorer Wilfred Thesiger, the controversial mystic Laurens van der Post, and the indefatigable Norman Lewis of *Naples '44*. Among these, Leigh Fermor shines with the élan and the effortlessly cultured glow of an apparent golden age. A war hero of polymathic exuberance, brilliant linguistic skills, and an elephantine memory, he was sometimes fancifully compared to Lord Byron or Sir Philip Sydney.

Two pairs of books came to exemplify his achievement. The first pair—*Mani* (1958) and *Roumeli* (1966)—celebrated the Greece that held his abiding fascination and where he lived for forty-five years on a once-wild promontory in the Peloponnese. In *Mani*, especially, he described this backwater region as a world whose way of life had survived in a fierce and enchanted time warp.

The land he depicted is barely recognizable now—tourism, he observed, destroys the object it loves—but it was less the Greece of classical antiquity that beguiled him than the spirit and folk culture of the hinterland: the earthy, demotic *Romiosyne* that he once contrasted with the Hellenic ideal in a playful balance sheet of the country's character.

In these, and in later books, the style was the man: robustly imaginative, cultivated without pedantry, unstoppably digressive, forgivably swanky, and filled with infectious learning. The impression—overflowing into elaborate footnotes and flights of learned fantasy—is one of omnivorous delight in the quirks and byways of history, art, language, genealogy, myth, song, superstition, costume, heraldry, and everything else that struck his fancy.

His literary models were Norman Douglas and Robert Byron, but his writing was more vivid than the one, more kindly than the other. Despite the richness of his prose (occasionally slipping into purple) he forged an illusion of intimacy with his readers, as if they were sharing his mind in the moment of writing. But in fact his manuscripts were worked, reworked, and reworked again with such painstaking perfectionism that his publisher (the benign Jock Murray) often had to reset his galley proofs wholesale. The apparently natural flow of words was in reality a densely worked choreography, which came at cost.

Fifteen years ago, swimming in the Ionian Sea beneath his home, where nobody could overhear us, Paddy (as friends and fans called him) suddenly confessed to me the writer's block that would plague the rest of his life. The expectations of a now-avid public, and his own obsessive perfectionism, were taking their toll, and he could not overleap this cruel impediment.

I remember him strong into old age. He swam every morning, with a sturdy breaststroke far out to sea, the tattoo of a twin-tailed mermaid glistening on his shoulder. He still kept up a striding march in the Taygetus foothills, where he and his wife Joan had designed their own house above the ocean. It was a place of "mad splendor," he wrote. Its sitting-room library—bookshelves banked nine feet high—opened onto a vista of cypresses and the Messenian Gulf, and was flagged with the greenish stone of Mount Pelion. In the afternoon Paddy would disappear into his study to confront—or escape—the demons of his failed writing, and would emerge to the liberation of ouzo or whiskey, generally to report some arcane piece of research—that the Huns wore stitched field-mouse skins, perhaps—or to share a passage of Ovid. We dined in the monastic half-cloister he had built beside his home, and once we visited the tiny, red-tiled Byzantine chapel where—five years before—he had buried the ashes of Bruce Chatwin.

The conflict between a natural gregariousness and the solitude of writing never quite resolved for him. In a short, intriguing study named *A Time to Keep Silence* (1953) he recorded his sojourn in three great French monasteries. He described this retreat not as a religious exercise, but as a need for a haven for writing, and the nature of its cleansing—"the troubled waters of the mind grow still and clear"—remains suspended like a question mark in the oeuvre of a man to whom self-revelation seemed indulgence.

The second pair of books, which established Paddy's primacy among travel writers, must be among the most extraordinary ever written. In 1933, as a youth of eighteen, he left England for a journey that would take a year and a half. As "a thousand glistening umbrellas were tilted over a thousand bowler hats in Piccadilly," he set out to walk to Constantinople (as he nostalgically called Istanbul). Walking stick in hand, a copy of Horace's Odes in his rucksack, he pursued a meandering course up the Rhine and down the Danube, across the Great Hungarian Plain, into Romania and through the Balkans to Turkey.

It was almost forty-five years before he published the first part of this journey, and another nine years before the second. *A Time of*

Gifts (1977) and *Between the Woods and the Water* (1986) represent prodigious feats of memory. They record the rite of passage of a precocious, exuberant young man as he encounters the peoples and languages of a Middle Europe now littered with obsolete names: Bohemia, Transylvania, Wallachia. His story must have become the dream journey of every enterprising and footloose adolescent.

Inevitably the accuracy of Paddy's memory was questioned, and he was frank about occasional imaginative license and conflation. (His first diary was stolen in Munich, a solitary last one recovered years later in Romania.) Certainly his recall was extraordinary. I remember the first time we met (by chance), when he quoted verbatim from my first book passages that I had myself forgotten. A year before his death we chanted verses from the *Rubáiyát* of Omar Khayyám together in an antiphonal competition (which he won).

His urge to describe his epic journey more than forty years after its end was a deeply natural one. He was revisiting his youthful persona with the judgment and knowledge of maturity; yet in a sense he had remained unchanged. Despite his sophisticated learning, he retained an almost boyish innocence, as if the troubles of the modern age had bypassed him. In the Peloponnese, where he settled to live in the 1960s, he had remained in thrall to a more ancient, rooted culture than that of the urban West.

The final volume of his proposed trilogy—carrying its author through the Balkans and down the Black Sea coast to Turkey—became his tormenting and elusive project for the next quarter-century, and was never completed. Some near-finished version, however, survives him, and will eventually be published.

With his youthful trek done, Leigh Fermor's career took off into near fable. Caught up in Greek unrest, he joined in a triumphal royalist cavalry charge against wilting Venizelist rebels. In Athens he fell in love with the artist Princess Balasha Cantacuzene, twelve years older than him, and lived with her in Moldavia for over two years, before World War II recalled him to London.

As a fluent Greek speaker he was recruited by the Intelligence Corps, and sent as a liaison officer with the Greek army first to Albania and finally to Crete, where he survived the brutal German invasion. For almost two years, while an officer in the Special Operations Executive, he lived disguised as a shepherd in the Cretan mountains, organizing the gathering of intelligence.

Then, in 1944, occurred the exploit that—more than any other— was to burnish him into legend. He and his fellow SOE officer Stanley Moss dreamed up a scheme of harebrained bravado. Dressed in stolen German uniforms, with a party of Cretan guerrillas, they ambushed the car of General Heinrich Kreipe, the German commander of occupied Crete, kidnapped him, and concealed him under the back seat. Moss took the wheel, Paddy donned the general's cap, and together they drove through twenty-two checkpoints to emerge on the far side of Herakleion and march Kreipe for three weeks over the mountains, to be picked up by motor launch and taken to Egypt.

It was during this hazardous Cretan march, as the dawn broke over Mount Ida, mythical birthplace of Zeus, that the abducted general began to murmur a verse of Horace: *Vides ut alta stet nive candidum/Soracte....*[1] It was an ode that Paddy knew by heart, and he completed the six stanzas to their end. "The general's blue eyes had swivelled away from the mountain-top to mine," Paddy later wrote,

—and when I'd finished, after a long silence, he said: "Ach so, Herr Major!" It was very strange. As though, for a long moment,

---

1. "See Mount Soracte white with snow...."

the war had ceased to exist. We had both drunk at the same fountains long before; and things were different between us for the rest of our time together.

This precocious kidnapping was later reimagined in a lackluster movie named *Ill Met by Moonlight* (1957) with Dirk Bogarde playing Paddy. But there were other exploits too. Paddy had already engineered the defection of the Italian General Angelico Carta from Crete; and he was due to undertake a near-suicidal mission to Colditz when the war ended.

His upbeat account of these events was tempered by regret. He had planned that the abduction of Kreipe be bloodless, but his accompanying Cretan partisans slit the chauffeur's throat, and rumors of grim German reprisals for the abduction have never quite died down. Above all, Paddy's accidental shooting of one of his fellow guerrillas may have stained his memory of the whole period.

On June 16 Leigh Fermor was buried back in the English countryside, attended by an Intelligence Corps guard of honor, to lie beside his wife Joan, his dear comrade since 1946. This was, in a sense, fitting. For in certain ways he was exemplary of a wartime Englishness now almost gone, whose more dashing qualities merged seamlessly into the hardy stylishness of Greek *leventéa*.

To those who knew him, his books are hauntingly redolent of his sensibility. His conversation was irrepressibly warm and inventive far into old age, moving from arcane anecdotes to fanciful wordplay or bursting into polyglot song (sometimes singing the lyrics backward). His friends ranged from Deborah, Duchess of Devonshire—last of the six legendary Mitford sisters (his correspondence with her was published in 2008[2])—to early acquaintance with a raffish interwar bohemia and his own great predecessor, the travel writer and aesthete Robert Byron, whose borrowed rucksack he bore across Central Europe as a youth.

Almost the last time I met Paddy, he had returned home after an operation for suspected cancer, and I feared he would be depleted, his old zest gone. He was growing deaf, and he suffered from tunnel vision (which he called Simplonitis). For a while, sitting over lunch, he seemed subdued. Then something struck him. He perked up, and said: "You know, there is an apple lying on a table in the hall. It's been there all weekend. Wouldn't it be marvelous if it cocked a snook at Newton, and simply took off into the air!"

This was typical of his boyish resilience. In the field of travel he evoked both the youthful wanderer who discovers another world and the avid scholar who melds with it. His prose was too rich and elaborate to be a safe influence on others (although a few have tried); but he brought to the genre not only the distinction of his densely brilliant books, but his innate dignity, ebullient mind, and capacious heart.

—September 29, 2011

---

2. The correspondence, *In Tearing Haste*, edited by Charlotte Mosley, was published in the US by New York Review Books (2010), which has also republished the other books by Patrick Leigh Fermor mentioned in this article, as well as *The Traveller's Tree*.

ABOUT THE AUTHORS AND SUBJECTS

ANNA AKHMATOVA (1889–1966) was a major figure in twentieth-century Russian poetry. Her poem cycle *Requiem* describes her experiences under the Stalinist terror.

NOEL ANNAN (1916–2000) was a British military intelligence officer and writer, and a frequent contributor to *The New York Review of Books*. His books include *Our Age: Portrait of a Generation* and *Changing Enemies: The Defeat and Regeneration of Germany*.

HANNAH ARENDT (1906–1975) was a German political theorist who, over the course of many books, explored themes such as violence, revolution, and evil. Her major works include *The Origins of Totalitarianism*, *The Human Condition*, and the controversial *Eichmann in Jerusalem*, in which she coined the phrase "the banality of evil."

W.H. AUDEN (1907–1973) was an English poet, playwright, and essayist who lived and worked in the United States for much of the second half of his life. His work, from his early strictly metered verse and plays written in collaboration with Christopher Isherwood to his later dense poems and penetrating essays, represents one of the major achievements of twentieth-century literature.

GEORGE BALANCHINE (1904–1983) was one of the most important choreographers of the twentieth century. Born in Russia, he fled to Paris in 1924 and came to the United States in 1934, where he remained for the rest of his life. He cofounded and was the balletmaster of the New York City Ballet and choreographed some four hundred ballets, working frequently with the composer Igor Stravinsky. His most famous works include *Apollo* for the Ballets Russes and *La Sonnambula*, *Jewels*, and *The Nutcracker* for the New York City Ballet.

ISAIAH BERLIN (1909–1997) was a political philosopher and historian of ideas. Born in Riga, he moved in 1917 with his family to Petrograd, where he witnessed the Russian Revolution. In 1921 he emigrated to England. He was educated at Oxford and became a Fellow of All Souls College, where he was later appointed Professor of Social and Political Theory. He served as the first president of Wolfson College, Oxford, and as president of the British Academy.

JOHN BERRYMAN (1914–1972) was an American poet whose major work was a series of interconnected poems entitled *The Dream Songs*. He taught at the Iowa Writers' Workshop and for many years at the University of Minnesota.

HECTOR BIANCIOTTI (1930–) is a French writer born in Argentina. He served as the Literary Correspondent for *Le Monde* and is the author of the novel *What the Night Tells the Day*, among others.

ELIZABETH BISHOP (1911–1979) was an American poet who traveled frequently throughout her life, living for significant periods of time in Key West and Brazil. She won the Pulitzer Prize and the National Book Award, and was the first woman to win the Neustadt International Prize for Literature. Her volumes of verse include *Poems: North & South/A Cold Spring*, *A Question of Travel*, and *Geography III*.

ELENA BONNER (1923–) is a human rights activist and the widow of Andrei Sakharov. She is the author of *Alone Together* and *Mothers and Daughters*.

JORGE LUIS BORGES (1899–1986) was an Argentine short-story writer, poet, and essayist. His fiction, which drew on his interest in mathematics and detective stories, among other things, made him one of the influential writers of the twentieth century. His stories were published in English in collections such as *Ficciones*, *The Aleph*, and *Labryinths*.

JOSEPH BRODSKY (1940–1996) was born in Leningrad and moved to the United States when he was exiled from Russia in 1972. His poetry collections include *A Part of Speech* and *To Urania*; his essay collections include *Less Than One*, which won the National Book Critics Circle Award, and *Watermark*. In 1987, he was awarded the Nobel Prize for Literature. He served as US Poet Laureate from 1991 to 1992.

LENNY BRUCE (1925–1966) was a comedian whose celebrated stand-up routines pushed against conventional boundaries of style and subject matter. After being arrested for obscenity in San Francisco in 1961 he was repeatedly arrested in cities throughout the United States, and was found guilty in New York City in 1964 after a much-publicized six-month trial.

IAN BURUMA (1951–) is the Henry R. Luce Professor at Bard College. His books include *Murder in Amsterdam: The Death of Theo Van Gogh and the Limits of Tolerance, Taming the Gods: Religion and Democracy on Three Continents*, and the novel *The China Lover.*

BRUCE CHATWIN (1940–1989) was a British travel writer and novelist. His books include *In Patagonia, The Viceroy of Ouidah*, and *On the Black Hill,* which won the James Tait Black Memorial Prize in 1982.

DOUGLAS COOPER (1911–1984) was a British art historian and art collector, mainly of Cubist paintings. He wrote extensively about Pablo Picasso, as well as monographs on Juan Gris, Paul Klee, and Henri de Toulouse-Lautrec, among others.

ARTHUR GOLD (1917–1990) and ROBERT FIZDALE (1920–1995) performed together for decades as a two-piano ensemble, playing works by composers including John Cage, Virgil Thomson, and Paul Bowles. They also wrote biographies of Sarah Bernhardt and Misia Sert and hosted a cooking show on television.

EDWARD GOREY (1925–2000) studied briefly at the Art Institute of Chicago, spent three years in the army testing poison gas, and attended Harvard College, where he majored in French literature and roomed with the poet Frank O'Hara. In 1953 Gorey published *The Unstrung Harp*, the first of his many books, which include *The Curious Sofa, The Haunted Tea Cosy*, and *The Epiplectic Bicycle*. In addition to illustrating his own books, Gorey provided drawings to countless books for both children and adults.

ELIZABETH HARDWICK (1916–2007) was born in Lexington, Kentucky, and educated at the University of Kentucky and Columbia University. A recipient of a Gold Medal from the American Academy of Arts and Letters, she was the author of three novels, a biography of Herman Melville, and four collections of essays. She was a cofounder and advisory editor of *The New York Review of Books*, to which she contributed more than one hundred reviews, articles, reflections, and letters.

ZBIGNIEW HERBERT (1924–1998) was a Polish poet, essayist, and playwright. His first poetry collection, *The Chord of Light*, was published in 1956, and the English translation of his *Selected Poems* in 1968 brought him international recognition.

AILEEN KELLY (1942–), a fellow of King's College, Cambridge, is the author of *Toward Another Shore: Russian Thinkers Between Necessity and Chance* and, most recently, *Views from the Other Shore: Essays on Herzen, Chekhov, and Bakhtin*.

MURRAY KEMPTON (1917–1997) was a columnist for *Newsday*, as well as a regular contributor to *The New York Review of Books*. His books include *Rebellions, Perversities, and Main Events*, *The Briar Patch*, and *Part of Our Time*. He won the Pulitzer Prize for Commentary in 1985.

IVAN KLÍMA (1931–) is a Czech novelist and playwright whose writing and life was shaped by his experiences in the Theresienstadt concentration camp with his family during World War II and under Czech communism. His books include the novels *Love and Garbage, No Saints or Angels*, and *The Ultimate Intimacy*.

PATRICK LEIGH FERMOR (1915–2011), called "the finest English travel writer of his generation," was born in 1915 of English and Irish descent. After his stormy schooldays, he walked across Europe to Constantinople. During the Second World War he served as a guerilla on the German-occupied island of Crete, disguised as a shepherd. There, he famously kidnapped the Nazi commander and spirited him out of the country, an exploit for which he was awarded a DSO. He was knighted in 2004.

ROBERT LOWELL (1917–1977) was twice awarded the Pulitzer Prize for

Poetry. *Life Studies, For the Union Dead,* and *The Dolphin* are among his many volumes of verse. He was a cofounder of and contributor to *The New York Review of Books.*

ALISON LURIE (1926–) is a former Professor of English at Cornell. Her novels include *Foreign Affairs,* which won the Pulitzer Prize for Fiction in 1984, *The War Between the Tates,* and *Truth and Consequences.*

NADEZHDA MANDELSTAM (1899–1980) was a Russian writer and the wife of the poet Osip Mandelstam. She published two memoirs about their lives under Stalinist repression, *Hope Against Hope* and *Hope Abandoned.*

OSIP MANDELSTAM (1891–1938) was born and raised in St. Petersburg. He first published his poems in *Apollyon,* an avant-garde magazine, in 1910, then formed the Acmeist group with Anna Akhmatova and Nicholas Gumilev. Unpopular with the Soviet authorities, Mandelstam found it increasingly difficult to publish his poetry, though an edition of his collected poems did come out in 1928. In 1934, after reading an epigram denouncing Stalin to friends, Mandelstam was arrested and sent into internal exile.

MARY MCCARTHY (1912–1989) was the author of the novels *The Group, The Groves of Academe,* and *Birds of America;* among her nonfiction books are *Venice Observed, The Stones of Florence, Vietnam,* and the autobiographies *Memories of a Catholic Girlhood* and *How I Grew. A Bolt from the Blue and Other Essays,* a collection of her literary, cultural, and political writings, was published by New York Review Books in 2002.

JAMES MERRILL (1926–1995) was an American poet whose major work *The Changing Light at Sandover* describes a series of spirit communications conducted over many years. He won the National Book Award for his collections *Nights and Days* and *Mirabell: Books of Number.*

ADAM MICHNIK (1946–) is Editor in Chief of the Warsaw daily newspaper *Gazeta Wyborcza.* He was an important figure in the democratic opposition that led to the end of Communist rule in Poland in 1989.

JONATHAN MILLER (1934–) has directed operas and plays throughout the world, including acclaimed productions of *Rigoletto, The Marriage of Figaro,* and *Pelléas and Mélisande.* His many books include *The Body in Question, States of Mind, On Reflection,* and *Nowhere in Particular.*

JONATHAN MIRSKY (1932–) is a historian and journalist specializing in Asian affairs. Until 1998 he was East Asia editor of *The Times* of London. In 1990 he was named International Journalist of the Year by the British Press Awards for his coverage of the Tiananmen uprising.

GEORGE ORTIZ is an American art collector with an extensive collection of artifacts and objects from around the world, with an emphasis on ancient and classical Greece.

BORIS PASTERNAK (1890–1960) was a Russian novelist and poet. He was awarded the Nobel Prize for Literature in 1958, but forced by the Soviet authorities to decline it. His novel *Doctor Zhivago* was an international sensation when published abroad but he was not allowed to publish it in the Soviet Union during his lifetime.

DARRYL PINCKNEY (1953–) is the author of a novel, *High Cotton,* and, in the Alain Locke Lecture Series, *Out There: Mavericks of Black Literature.* He is a frequent contributor to *The New York Review of Books.*

DAWN POWELL (1896–1965) was an American novelist and short-story writer who lived in Greenwich Village in New York City for most of her life. Her novels include *My Home is Far Away, The Locusts Have No King,* and *The Golden Spur.*

JOHN RICHARDSON (1924–) is a British art historian. The first three volumes of his biography of Pablo Picasso were published in 1991, 1996, and 2007. He is currently at work on Volume Four.

PHILIP ROTH (1933–) is an American novelist born in Newark, New Jersey, which has served as the setting for many of his novels. He won the National Book Award for his first book, *Goodbye, Columbus,* and for *Sabbath's*

Theater, the Pulitzer Prize for *American Pastoral*, and three PEN/Faulkner awards, for *Operation Shylock*, *The Human Stain*, and *Everyman*.

ANDREI SAKHAROV (1921–1989) was a Soviet nuclear physicist, author, and human rights activist. He won the Nobel Peace Prize in 1975.

JOHN SCHLESINGER (1926–2003) was an English film and stage director. His best-known films include *Midnight Cowboy*, which won Oscars for Best Picture and Best Director, *The Day of the Locust*, and *Marathon Man*.

FRANK SINATRA (1915–1998) was internationally renowned as one of the greatest American popular singers of the twentieth century.

STEPHEN SPENDER (1909–1995) was an English poet and essayist. As a young man he became friends with W.H. Auden, Louis MacNeice, Cecil Day-Lewis, and Christopher Isherwood, a loose collection often referred to as "the Auden Group" or "MacSpaunday." He published many collections of poems, including *The Still Centre* and *Ruins and Visions*, and numerous volumes of nonfiction and other works, including *Learning Laughter* and *Love-Hate Relations*.

GERTRUDE STEIN (1874–1946) was an American writer and patron of the arts who lived in Paris for most of her life. She was an early supporter of Cubism and was interested in applying its theories to her writing. Her works include the novel *The Making of Americans*, the poetry collection *Tender Buttons*, *The Autobiography of Alice B. Toklas*, and two opera librettos scored by Virgil Thomson, *Four Saints in Three Acts* and *The Mother of Us All*.

SAUL STEINBERG (1914–1999) was a Romanian born cartoonist and illustrator famous for his witty drawings and paintings for *The New Yorker*.

JOHN THOMPSON (1918–2002) was Robert Lowell's friend and roommate at Kenyon College and the author of *The Founding of English Meter*.

VIRGIL THOMSON (1896–1989) was a modernist American composer and music critic. His many works include the operas *Four Saints in Three Acts*,

The Mother of Us All, and *Lord Byron*, film scores for *The River* and *The Spanish Earth*, and many other works for orchestra and voice.

COLIN THUBRON (1939–) is a travel writer and novelist. His travel books include *Mirror to Damascus*, *Among the Russians*, *Behind the Wall*, which won the Thomas Cook Travel Award and the Hawthornden prize, *The Lost Heart of Asia*, and *In Siberia*. His fiction includes *The God in the Mountain*, *Emperor*, *A Cruel Madness*, which won the Silver Pen award, *Falling*, *Turning Back the Sun*, *Distance*, and *To the Last City*. His latest book is *To a Mountain in Tibet*. In 2000 he was awarded the Mungo Park Medal, and the Lawrence of Arabia Memorial Medal in 2001.

JOHN UPDIKE (1932–2009) was born in Shillington, Pennsylvania. In 1954 he began to publish in *The New Yorker*, to which he continued to contribute short stories, poems, and criticism until his death. He also wrote frequent art criticism for *The New York Review of Books*. His major work was the set of four novels chronicling the life of Harry "Rabbit" Angstrom, the final two of which, *Rabbit is Rich* and *Rabbit at Rest*, won the Pulitzer Prize for Fiction.

GORE VIDAL (1925–) is an American novelist, essayist, and playwright. His many works include the memoirs *Point to Point Navigation* and *Palimpsest*, the novels *The City and the Pillar*, *Myra Breckinridge*, and *Lincoln*, and the collection *United States: Essays 1952–1992*.